Journal of the
INDIAN WARS

Volume One, No. 3

Savas Publishing Company

202 First Street SE, Suite 103A, Mason City, IA 50401

Subscription and Publishing Information

Journal of the Indian Wars (*JIW*) is published quarterly by Savas Publishing Company, 202 First Street SE, Suite 103A, Mason City, IA 50401. Publisher: Theodore P. Savas. (515) 421-7135 (voice); (515)-421-8370 (fax); E-mail: cwbooks@mach3ww.com. Our online military history catalog of original books is found at www.savaspublishing.com.

SUBSCRIPTIONS to *JIW* are available at $29.95/yr. (four books); Canada and overseas is $39.95/yr. Write to: Savas Publishing Company, *JIW* Subscriptions, 202 First Street SE, Suite 103A, Mason City, IA 50401. Check, MO, MC or V accepted. Phone, fax or E-mail orders welcome. All subscriptions begin with the current issue unless otherwise specified.

DISTRIBUTION in North America is handled by Peter Rossi at Stackpole Books, 5067 Ritter Road, Mechanicsburg, PA 17055-6921. 800-732-3669 (voice); 717-976-0412 (fax); E-mail: prossi@stackpolebooks.com. European distribution is through Greenhill Books, Park House, 1 Russell Gardens, London NW11 9NN, England; E-mail: LionelLeventhal@compuserve.com; Back issues of *JIW* are available through Stackpole Books or your local bookseller. Retail price is $11.95 plus shipping ($4.00 for the first book and $1.00 for each additional book). Check, money order, MC/V, AE, or D are accepted. Contact Stackpole Books for quantity discounts.

MANUSCRIPTS, REVIEWS, AND NEWS SUBMISSIONS are welcome. For guidelines, consult our web site (www.savaspublishing.com) or send a self-addressed stamped envelope to Michael A. Hughes, Editor, *Journal of the Indian Wars*, 834 East Sixth Street, Box E, Ada, OK 74820. Proposals for articles (recommended) should include a brief description of your topic, a list of primary sources, and estimate of completion date. Manuscripts should be accompanied by a 3.5" disk with copies in both WordPerfect 6.1 (or lower) and Rich Text (RTF) formats. Persons interested in reviewing books should send a description of their qualifications, areas of expertise, and desired titles and topics. News submissions should include a brief abstracted version of any information. Submitted news may be posted on our web site at our discretion. Enclose a SASE if requesting a reply and include your E-mail and fax number. Publications (which may include page proofs) and videos for potential review should be sent to the managing editor.

JIW is published with the cooperation of Jerry Russell and the Order of the Indian Wars. Without Jerry's non-too-gentle proddings and earnest supplications, it would not have come to fruition. For more information, please write to OIW, P.O. Box 7401, Little Rock AR 72217.

Savas Publishing Company

Publisher
Theodore P. Savas

Editorial Assistants: Patrick Bowmaster, William Haley
Graphics: Jim Zach
Marketing: Nancy Lund
Indexing: Lee W. Merideth

Journal of the Indian Wars

Managing Editor: Michael A. Hughes
Associate Editors: Patrick Bowmaster, Rod Thomas,
Phil Konstantin, and Eril B. Hughes
Book Review Editor: Patrick Jung
Advertising/Circulation: Carol A. Savas
Editorial Consultants: Brian Pohanka,
Jerry Keenan, Neil Mangum, Jerry Russell, and Ted Alexander

Civil War Regiments Journal

Managing Editor: Theodore P. Savas

Assistant Editors: Lee Merideth, William Haley
Circulation/Advertising: Carol Savas
Book Review Editor: Archie McDonald

Contributors

Paul N. Beck is an associate professor of U. S. and military history at Wisconsin Lutheran College in Milwaukee, Wisconsin.

Palmer Boeger is a retired professor of history and a former national park interpreter who still instructs in military history at East Central University in Ada, Oklahoma. He has published articles and books on Oklahoma history.

Patrick Bowmaster, an historical researcher with Mary Baker Eddy Collections and Library in Boston, is an associate editor of *Journal of the Indian Wars*.

Ellen Farrell is a graduate assistant in the American Studies Program at the University of Minnesota—Minneapolis.

Dave Gjeston recently retired from the Wisconsin Department of Natural Resources. He planned the restoration of the Black Hawk War battlefield of Wisconsin Heights to its historic appearance.

Michael Hughes is the managing editor of *Journal of the Indian Wars* and an instructor in art history, humanities, and history at [Oklahoma] East Central University. He also leads a variety of art, archaeology, and history tours.

Charles Douglas Keller has been an interpreter at Little Bighorn National Battlefield, and is now posted at Pea Ridge National Military Park in Arkansas.

Colonel Rodney G. Thomas, an associate editor with *JIW*, retired from the U.S. Army in 1999 and now works for Pacific Environmental Services in North Carolina's Research Triangle.

Journal of the INDIAN WARS

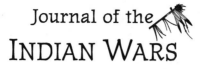

Table of Contents

continued

Table of Contents (continued)

FOREWORD

Theodore P. Savas

Our decision to explore obscure and misunderstood battles east of the Mississippi River in the last issue of *Journal of the Indian Wars* struck a chord with our readers. Many wrote or called to thank us for "straying from the beaten path" and "daring to publish something new and fresh." The presentation of original scholarship in an enjoyable format is the goal of *JIW*, and we are pleased to learn that you believe we are meeting our objective. We hope you find the articles in this compendium are no exception.

Most readers of Civil War and Indian War history know that a small force of Indians participated in the Battle of Pea Ridge; John Pope was banished to Minnesota after his disastrous performance at Second Bull Run to face the rebellious Sioux; Stand Watie and Ely Parker rose to high rank in the Confederate and Union armies, respectively; and a region labeled simply "Indian Territory" existed somewhere in the Trans-Mississippi Theater. All true. Yet the situation of American Indians during the Civil War period was much more complex, their fate more devastating and far-reaching than most students appreciate. Each of the articles in this issue underscore this point.

The 1862 Dakota War in Minnesota is often presented in black and white moral terms, with the Sioux receiving much of the blame for the killing of innocents. According to authors Paul Beck and Ellen Farrell, however, the origins of this war were complex, its results calamitous, and its consequences misunderstood. "Many historians have noted the escalation of hostilities between the Indians and the United States that accompanied the replacement of Regular troops" with volunteers, explains Beck. The state troops were indeed often more aggressive and likely to battle Indians than the regulars, but no blame for the bloodshed can be placed on the shoulders of the Minnesota Volunteers. In "Fair but Firm: The Minnesota Volunteers and the Coming of the

Dakota War of 1862," Beck explores the origins and fatal missteps that led to the killing of Dakota and whites alike. This fresh perspective on the origins of the conflict is complemented by Ellen Farrell's study, "The Most Terrible Stories: The 1862 Dakota Conflict in White Imagination." According to Farrell, "Two assumptions dominated all white discussions of [these] events. The first was that the attacks represented an act of Indian unity. . . . The second . . . was that the Dakota were uniformly and without exception guilty of unprovoked atrocities. Farrell's essay debunks both of these misconceptions.

Stand Watie's name may be known to most Civil War students, but his exploits remain largely ignored or misunderstood. "Chiefs by Commission: Stand Watie and Ely Parker," by Patrick Bowmaster, introduces readers to Watie and Parker through a detailed biographical sketch of both men. Palmer Boeger builds on Pat's foundation by exploring the Confederate Cherokee officer's role in two actions during the Civil War. "Flowing With Blood and Whiskey: Stand Watie and the Battles of First and Second Cabin Creek," demonstrates that the daring cavalry officer excelled at raiding tactics. His combined effort with General Richard Gano against a Federal wagon train at Second Cabin Creek in 1864 also demonstrates Watie's solid command abilities in a pitched action. The battle did not change the course of the war, writes Boeger, but "Second Cabin Creek stands as the Confederacy's most significant victory in the Indian Territory and one of the greatest Confederate triumphs in the Trans-Mississippi West."

Editor Michael A. Hughes's contribution to this issue reminds readers that the impact of the Civil War on Indians across the nation was devastating, and its impact long-lasting. Indeed, writes Hughes, its consequences, in many cases, are still being felt today. "Nations Asunder: The Western American Indians in the Civil War, 1861-1865," presents a sweeping overview of the history, geography, experiences, and significance of the war's impact on a large number of Indian "nations" from New England to California. "One reason for the obscurity of the 1860s' Indian wars," explains Hughes, "is that many of them took place within the overwhelming context of the American Civil War." As Michael's encyclopedic essay drives home, "dozens of native nations were either swept up in the great contest or were participants in smaller but no less disastrous conflicts." The sheer scope and brutality of what was happening across this country to Native Americans will surprise and sicken even the most well-read students of the Civil War.

Several other contributions close out this issue of *JIW*. This quarter's featured interview introduces our readers to Doug Keller, battlefield interpreter at Pea Ridge, Arkansas. Doug, who has been a strong supporter of *JIW*, offers interesting insights into Indian and Civil War history. The issue of whether Indians scalped Union soldiers at Pea Ridge is finally put to rest—and Doug now has enough information to actually *identify by name* many of the scalped troops.

Our last issue contained an in-depth "reconsideration" of the Black Hawk War. As a follow-up, this month's featured travel article is Dave Gjeston's "Wisconsin's 1832 Black Hawk Trail." According to Gjeston, historical markers tracing Black Hawk's path through Wisconsin are now in place, "enabling visitors to travel the route and learn of the events."

Rodney Thomas rounds out this issue with his popular column "Thomas Online." This quarter, Rod focuses his attention on a virtually unknown topic: women warriors. Their records were heroic, explains Rod, "but they have often been relegated to mere mentions in footnotes and their deeds labeled irrelevant." This obscurity is unfortunate, since it presents an incomplete portrait of Native American history. As usual, Rod offers numerous sources for further reading.

We thank you for your continued support, encouragement, and contributions.

"Firm but Fair"

THE MINNESOTA VOLUNTEERS
AND THE COMING OF THE
DAKOTA WAR OF 1862

Paul N. Beck

S ome died by fire, some by water. Twelve soldiers lay dead of gunfire with the first flare of muzzle blasts at the ferry landing. As their surviving comrades retreated, eleven more volunteers were felled by Dakota bullets, and their commander sank while struggling in the waters of the Minnesota River. Tragically, the men who had tried the hardest to prevent the war that was erupting were among its first victims.

A little after 10:00 a.m. on August 18, 1862, J. C. Dickinson, a local settler, stumbled into Fort Ridgely with the startling news that the Dakota "Sioux" had attacked the Lower Sioux Agency. The Indians had already killed many of the agency's civilian employees, as well as traders and their families. The commander at the fort, Capt. John Marsh, reacted promptly. Within a short time he had assembled a relief column of Minnesota volunteer troops and marched out of the fort prepared to quell the fighting.[1]

Marsh was confident that the attack on the agency was a small matter that could easily be put right. He had, after all, defused a similar volatile situation just weeks before at the Upper Sioux Agency. Peter Quinn, the seventy-five-year-old post interpreter, was not as positive as Marsh; before leaving the fort with the relief force, Quinn bid a solemn good-bye to several friends.[2]

The Lower Sioux Agency lay roughly thirteen miles from Fort Ridgely and across the Minnesota River. Marsh and Quinn, mounted on mules and accompanied by forty-six men of Company B of the Fifth Minnesota Infantry Regiment riding in wagons, traveled to the Redwood Ferry, located one mile from the agency. Along the way, the soldiers encountered dozens of fleeing civilians, who spoke of the horror of the Dakota war parties, homes burned and loved ones murdered. The survivors warned Marsh to return to the fort, but he refused. Marsh held a low opinion of Indian military skill and bravery. He also believed he held the respect and fear of the Dakota leaders and that his presence would soon restore order. He was sadly mistaken. Within a few hours one-half of his command would be killed in an ambush at the Redwood Ferry.

The men of Marsh's detachment were among the first casualties of the Dakota War of 1862, the first major Indian war to occur in the West during the American Civil War.[3] The conflict would be followed by fighting in the Southwest, Pacific Northwest, and all across the Great Plains. There were serious conflicts with the Navajo, Apache and many of the Plains tribes. These struggles were often marked by military brutality and vicious atrocities like the Sand Creek Massacre. The fighting was so severe between 1862 and 1865 that historian Alvin Josephy remarked, "more Indian tribes were destroyed by whites and more land was seized from them [during this time] than in almost any comparable period of time in American history."[4]

Many historians have noted the escalation of hostilities between the Indians and the United States that accompanied the replacement of Regular troops sent east to fight the Confederates with 15,000 to 20,000 volunteer soldiers. From the end of the Mexican War to the start of the Civil War, several thousand Federal troops patrolled the vast regions of the West. They attempted to uphold the directives of the federal government to protect white settlers, keep whites from encroaching on Indian lands, arrest whiskey traders selling alcohol to the Indians, and uphold the treaties signed with the various tribes—treaties intended to keep the peace. Despite exhibiting some biases and slipping in a few glaring failures, the Regular Army had performed its responsibilities well, following a "firm but fair" policy. Historians have often seen the troops as a barrier protecting vulnerable Indians both from other Indian groups and greedy, racist whites. Brad Agnew, author of *Fort Gibson: Terminal on the Trail of Tears*, saw the Regulars as serving "not as the shock troops of white expansion but rather as a cultural buffer between whites and Indians."[5] The attack on Fort

Sumter in the spring of 1861 brought great upheaval to the frontier not the least of which was the replacing of professional soldiers with volunteer troops.

These volunteer soldiers, most of whom came from western states or territories, often paid little heed to federal Indian policies. To them, those standards were championed by a distant national government which during the war seemed apathetic about their local crises. Historians writing about the West during the Civil War era have argued that the state and territorial troops held a more negative and antagonistic view of Indians than did the Regulars. Robert Utley, an important historian of the Indian Wars, found that the volunteer army was more experienced with the frontier and its Indians, better motivated to confront them, and more aggressive, with a "a simpler, harder view of the Indian and the Indian problem than the regular force it replaced." He believed the volunteers were inclined to favor war over peace and more likely to fight rather than talk. "Less frequently now," wrote Utley, "did the army take the Indian side of a dispute or discriminate between shades of guilt, or seek solutions other then armed might. . . ." Other historians echo Utley's interpretation. Alvin Josephy agrees that the volunteers serving in the West "were tougher and harder on the tribes than the prewar Regulars had been." Likewise, Duane Schultz felt the volunteers were aggressive and militaristic because they held the belief that they fought to protect their home and families. Finally, T. R. Fehrenbach argued that the volunteers took the Indian wars "personally," a situation which led to "a series of slaughters and counter massacres, in all out ethnic warfare."[6]

The accuracy of these historians' statements, in general, cannot be denied; however, they cannot accurately be applied to the Minnesota volunteer soldiers and their role in the coming of the Dakota War of 1862. When listing the many and varied causes for the outbreak of war in southern Minnesota, one cannot place blame upon the Minnesota volunteers. Rather than provoking hostilities, the Minnesota troops strove to avoid conflict. In this they reflected attitudes and emulated the efforts of the Regulars they replaced at Fort Ridgely in the summer of 1861. By that time, the Regular Army had been serving for eight years at Fort Ridgely, located on the north bank of the Minnesota River in southeastern Minnesota. Its garrison was there to protect white settlers in the area, oversee the Dakota reservation and uphold the provisions of treaties signed with the Dakotas in 1851 and 1858.

The Dakota or "Santee" consisted of four bands—the Sisseton, Wahpeton, Wahpekute and Mdewakanton. Numbering some 8,000, the Dakota people were the easternmost of the powerful Sioux-speaking Indians. During most of the 1800s, the Dakota were semi-nomadic, traveling during certain times of the year before returning to their permanent villages, with an economy based on agriculture, gathering, hunting and trading furs to the whites. With 150,000 whites moving into Minnesota by the mid 1850s, the Dakota found themselves under heavy pressure to sell their lands and accept a reservation. Heavily in debt to white traders and with game becoming scarce, the Dakota reluctantly agreed to sign treaties with the federal government in 1851. These agreements divested the Dakota of over 25 million acres of land in present-day Minnesota, Iowa and South Dakota. In return, the Santee received a 150-mile-long, 10-mile wide reservation along the southern banks of the Minnesota River and a cash annuity payable over fifty years.[7] The displaced Dakota moved to their new reservation in 1853. Two Indian agencies, the Lower and Upper Sioux, and Fort Ridgely were built on the reservation during that year. The Lower Sioux Agency was located thirteen miles from the fort, while the Upper Sioux Agency was roughly fifty miles farther up the Minnesota River.[8]

Because of the proximity of the agencies to Fort Ridgely, there was considerable interaction between the Regular soldiers and the Dakota. Army officers at the fort held the usual racial biases of white Americans of the 1800s. They found the Dakota aggressive and warlike, disapproved of the perceived laziness of Sioux men, and firmly believed in the inevitability of their eventual assimilation into white civilization. As one officer wrote, "They have no alternatives . . . [but] to adopt civilized and industrious habits and live" or remain as they were, soon to die either "by famine or the sword." Yet, even though the officers were prejudiced and saw the Dakota as savage and inferior, they did not exhibit any real hatred toward the Sioux. In fact, the soldiers were among the few whites in the area who were concerned with the horrible conditions on the reservation and who showed sympathy for the Dakota.[9]

With its garrisons in such close contact with numerous Indian tribes, the army developed a policy on how to deal with them soon after it began occupying new forts in the West. This was especially important as the small Regular Army spread out across the frontier into the newly conquered territory gained from the Mexican-American War. Raised to believe that all Indians were savage and militant, and being greatly outnumbered by them, officers concluded that the only way to control relations with Indians was to be "firm, but fair." "Firm" meant being consistent in its dealings with the Indians and swift in punishing any violations of the peace. "Fair" implied that the military would be evenhanded when mediating situations involving whites and Indians and when upholding the treaties made between the federal government and Indians. At Fort Ridgely the Regular Army actually followed this firm but fair approach.

Time and again, soldiers from the fort crossed to the reservation at the request of the Indian agents to demonstrate the government's firmness to the Dakota. This seemed necessary to the agents as conditions on the reservation were deteriorating rapidly in the years prior to the Civil War. So many settlers had moved into the Minnesota River valley that hunting game became difficult. Dakota culture was under assault from missionaries and Indian agents, and the federal government's annuity system was so rife with corruption that greedy traders and government officials were able to steal most of the money owed to the Dakota for sale of their lands, leaving them hungry and destitute.[10] Rising tensions on the reservation, especially when an annuity payment was made, nearly led to violence with whites on several occasions. In response to pleas from Indian agents, detachments arrived from Fort Ridgely to restore order and keep the peace. The presence of the army and the threat of military action always forced the Dakota leaders to control their men and accept the injustices forced upon them.[11]

However, in their efforts to be fair, the Regulars often protected Dakota rights. White settlers tended to disregard reservation boundaries and sometimes moved illegally onto Dakota lands. Patrols from Fort Ridgely repeatedly removed them, sometimes forcibly, to the displeasure of the civilian population. When whites tried to smuggle illegal alcohol onto the reservation, the army sent out detachments to stop the sale of liquor. But it was the mistreatment of the Dakota by the Indian agents and white traders that brought forth the most protests from the army. "They have been on the verge of actual starvation," observed an officer from the fort while at the reservation, "paying to the traders forty-five dollars per head for lean beef cattle to keep their children from crying to them for food."

The economic exploitation of the Dakota by traders was not the only complaint the soldiers had with the administration of the reservation. Officers believed many Indian agents to be inept, ignorant of Indian culture, and corrupt. Such feelings were heartfelt by the soldiers at Fort Ridgely. They complained of agents who rarely spent time on the reservation and who had rotten food unfit for human consumption distributed to the Dakota.[12] Since 1849, when the newly created Department of the Interior replaced the War Department as administrator of Indian affairs, the army protested civilian control over the reservations. To them it was better that the reservations be supervised by honest military men. [13]

Dakota leaders, struggling to protect their people, quickly realized that there was friction between the reservation officials and the military and attempted to use it to their advantage. Many times, they journeyed to Fort Ridgely to protest the poor conditions on the reservations. At the post, the Dakota found sympathetic officers who accepted the truth of their allegations and often supported them against the agents and traders. Officers sent food to the agencies and supported Dakota rights in their letters to various government officials. If not exactly regarded as allies, Dakota leaders did view the soldiers as a possible source of justice as their world continued to collapse around them. [14]

The Santees' world was again disturbed when the Civil War started in 1861. The various units and regiments of the Regular Army were ordered to the East to fight. All across the West, white civilians became alarmed when the Regulars left their posts for the war in the East. Settlers envisioned Indian raids and massacres and demanded military protection. Whites living on the Minnesota frontier were no different; local newspapers reported rumors of Indian disturbances and called upon the government to reoccupy Fort Ridgely. [15] The federal government responded to the requests of western settlers and authorized the formation of state and territorial units to man the forts and posts left vacant by the Regulars. At different times between June 1861 and August 1862, companies of the First, Second, Fourth, and Fifth Minnesota Infantry Regiment garrisoned Fort Ridgely. No one—not the Dakota, reservation officials, nor even the volunteer soldiers themselves—knew how this would affect Indian-white relations in the Minnesota valley.

Many of the new soldiers came from towns like St. Paul and Glencoe, located close to the Minnesota River valley. These communities were less than fifty miles from the fort, so the men knew the area and the Dakota Indians firsthand. Many of the volunteers were frustrated with their assignment to places like Fort Ridgely. They had enlisted to fight to save the Union and crush the Southern rebellion; instead, they were ordered to the frontier to oversee the Dakota reservation. Lieutenant Thomas Gere of the Fifth Minnesota Infantry spoke for many of the volunteers when he wrote, "Have we done the country any good?"[16]

As noted earlier, civilian soldiers like Gere were usually unlike the Regulars they replaced. For one thing, they were not as well trained. The volunteers knew little of weaponry and drill, and their officers were mostly amateurs with little or no military training. In addition, the state volunteers differed from the Federal Regulars in that they held the views of the area settlers. They believed that the land belonged to whites, who they felt would make better use of it, and that its occupation by Indians was a problem of frontier life to be overcome in the same manner as   drought, insects and loneliness. These Minnesota soldiers may not have liked serving at Fort Ridgely, but they still felt possessive towards the valley it guarded. Lieutenant Timothy Sheehan, Fifth Minnesota, summed it up well in his journal when he noted that he found the "country along the Minnesota River a beautiful country, too good for Indians to inhabit."[17] Such attitudes increased tensions with the Dakota.

Indians frequently came to the fort to trade and observe the activities of the new garrison, and soldiers often journeyed to the reservation. The volunteers and the Dakota came away singularly unimpressed with one another. Captain Marsh was contemptuous of Sioux skill and bravery; Lt. Clark Kayser believed Indians were not the equal of white men, and he distrusted them. Lieutenant Sheehan and others showed little compassion for the nearly starved Dakota. When compared to the Regular soldiers they had come to know, the Dakota found the volunteers wanting. The Santee had little regard for soldiers who were few in number, unhappy with their duties, poorly trained, and disrespectful of Indians.[18]

But even though relations between the volunteers and the Dakota may not have been cordial, they remained surprisingly tranquil when compared with clashes that were occurring farther west. Along the frontier, much of the volunteer army was proving, as Utley called it, "aggressive and militant" toward Indians. In Nevada, captured Shoshone were mysteriously shot "while trying to escape." At Fort Fauntleroy in the New Mexico Territory, a friendly horse race between the garrison and local Navajo ended in a massacre, with soldiers brutally killing men, women and children. Before starting a campaign against the Mescalero Apaches, Brig. Gen. James H. Carleton issued an order to his field commanders: "All Indian men of that tribe are to be killed whenever and wherever you can find them."[18] On numerous occasions, volunteers provoked hostile actions with Indians. Yet the Minnesota soldiers, almost

Brigadier General
James H. Carleton

Generals in Blue

uniquely, tried to follow the "firm but fair" approach employed by the Regulars despite their personal biases.

After garrisoning Fort Ridgely, the Minnesota volunteers continued to perform the duties carried out by the Regulars they replaced. They removed settlers from the reservation and patrolled the area in an effort to arrest whiskey traders attempting to sell alcohol to the Dakota. They also tried to dispel the fears of area civilians and to determine the truth or falsehood of rumors about the Dakota. Soldiers from the fort were kept busy on expeditions sent out to confirm or dispel rumors by settlers of Dakota wrongdoing.[20] This prevented the organization of units that were even less professional than those of the volunteer regiments. For example, citizens of Mankato, a town located in the Minnesota valley, wanted to raise two militia or vigilante companies for frontier defense.

But several serious issues on the reservation were beyond the control of the volunteers, and those would soon lead to war. These difficulties included the arrival of a new Indian agent, the continued greed of the traders, and the tardiness of the annual annuity payments. The new agent, Thomas J. Galbraith, was not respected or liked by the Dakota. He was a typical political appointee, rewarded with a government position for his support of the Republican Party in the 1860 Presidential election. Galbraith knew nothing of the Indians and their culture and cared little about them. He was also arrogant, opinionated, and slow to take advice. Little Crow, one of the key leaders of the impending uprising, believed Galbraith's appointment to be one of the main factors leading to the war. Interestingly, Lieutenant Sheehan, who knew Galbraith, agreed with Little Crow and would write "my opinion is the same."[21]

A more serious grievance, causing greater resentment, was the greed and callousness of the white traders living on the reservation. Licensed by the government, they held a monopoly over Indian trade. With their lack of competition and political influence, the traders were able by fraud and manipulation to obtain thousands of dollars of the annuity money paid to the Dakota for their lands. The traders sold inferior goods at inflated prices, extending credit at high rates of interest when the Santee ran out of money. When the annuities arrived, the traders would stride boldly to the front of the payment line demanding that the ever-increasing debts owed to them by the long-suffering Dakota be paid first. Over the years, because of the greed of the traders, the Dakota received less and less of their annuity money, and their nation slowly began to starve. With the valley being swiftly populated by white farmers, the game with which the Dakota traditionally fed themselves was disappearing, making them increasingly dependent upon the annuity payments. Seeing the traders brazenly seizing upon much of the money needed to feed their women and children left Dakota men bitter and angry.[22]

By the summer of 1862, conditions on the reservation reached a crisis level. The previous winter had been a severe one, so cold that little hunting and gathering could be accomplished. In the spring, an infestation of cutworms ate its way ravenously through the Dakota cornfields. Forced to eat their horses and dogs and to grub for roots, the Sioux desperately needed the annuity money due to arrive in June 1862. Unfortunately, because of the Civil War raging back east, the payment was late.[23]

Although concerned with the delay of their money, Dakota leaders were even more afraid of what actions the traders would take once the payments did arrive. They feared that when the annuity money arrived, the traders would take virtually all of it in payment for old debts. Unable to get any support from the weak-willed Galbraith, a delegation of Dakota went to Fort Ridgely. There they turned to the members of the garrison, for the soldiers at Fort Ridgely had been their supporters in their struggles with the agents and traders.[23] But this time, they would not be greeted by officers of the Regular Army; instead the Dakota had to ask the volunteers for assistance. As they walked through the main gates of the post, Dakota leaders must have wondered what the response would be.

The Indian delegation was met by members of Company B, Fifth Minnesota Infantry Regiment. Company B had been stationed at Fort Ridgely since April 1862. Recruited from southeastern Minnesota, most of the men hailed from Filmore County. Their commanding officer was Capt. John Marsh. Marsh was a reasonable, confident man and an easygoing, popular officer. He was also one of the few men at the fort who actually had seen combat. Before being elected first lieutenant in the newly raised Fifth Regiment, Marsh had served for ten months with the Second Wisconsin Infantry Regiment and had seen action at the Battle of Bull Run.[25]

Marsh greeted the delegation warmly and listened to their complaints about the traders. The Dakota spoke of their concern that the traders would take their annuity and asked Marsh if the army would support this theft. Marsh assured them that he would not aid the traders, saying, "My boys are soldiers, not collecting agents for the traders." The delegation returned to the reservation relieved and more confident about receiving the upcoming payment.[26] Instead of acting in the bellicose manner of many volunteer officers serving in the West, who never believed or supported any Indian, Marsh accepted the complaints of the Dakota as truthful; like the Regular officers who had been at the post before him, he promised to be fair with the Sioux. But the commitment of the volunteer officers and men to the "firm but fair" policy was soon tested with a critical situation at the Upper Sioux Agency.

Several thousand members of the Sisseton and Wahpeton bands of the Dakota were waiting at the Upper Sioux Agency for the annuity payment. The traders, knowing that the funds were late and still furious at Marsh for supporting the Indians, refused to extend the Dakota more credit. When a delegation of Dakota went to Galbraith to request that he distribute the food and provisions portion of the annuity that was already stored in government warehouses, they received a blunt refusal. Galbraith's response was an order for them to disperse their people and come back in a month. Fearful of the resentment this caused, Galbraith wrote to Superintendent of Indian Affairs Clark Thompson, and asked that soldiers be sent to the Upper Sioux Agency.[27]

A detachment of 100 men from Companies B and C of the Fifth Minnesota arrived at the agency on July 2. Lieutenant Thomas Gere, second in command, was a jovial, well-liked nineteen-year-old, elected to his position only months earlier. Lieutenant Timothy Sheehan, a serious twenty-five-year-old Irishman, commanded the force. Within days of arriving at the agency, Sheehan realized that he and his small command were in a dangerous position. By then, some 5,000 Dakota had reassembled at the agency. They were still starving, the traders still refused credit, and the payment had still not arrived. The Dakota were desperate and angry. If hostilities erupted, Sheehan and his men would easily be overwhelmed and killed. Afraid that this would happen, the agency minister prayed to God to "help them and spare their lives."[28]

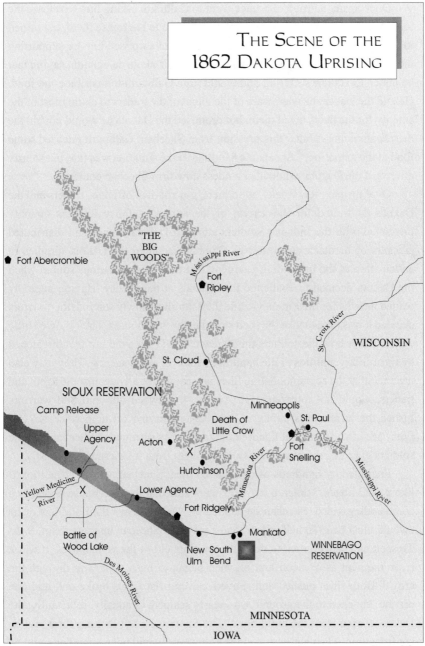

THE SCENE OF THE
1862 DAKOTA UPRISING

Fort Abercrombie

"THE BIG WOODS"

Mississippi River

Fort Ripley

St. Croix River

WISCONSIN

St. Cloud

SIOUX RESERVATION

Camp Release

Upper Agency

Acton

Minneapolis

St. Paul

Death of Little Crow

Fort Snelling

Yellow Medicine River

Hutchinson

Lower Agency

Minnesota River

Mississippi River

Fort Ridgely

Battle of Wood Lake

Mankato

New Ulm

South Bend

WINNEBAGO RESERVATION

Des Moines River

MINNESOTA

IOWA

Theodore P. Savas

Once again, a group of Santee went to Galbraith asking him to release the food stored in the warehouses. Galbraith still wanted to refuse them, but turned to Sheehan and asked his opinion. The lieutenant surprised him by supporting the Dakota. Sheehan expressed sympathy to the Dakota delegation, saying that he understood their suffering and would urge Galbraith to distribute the food. He told the leaders he was aware of the intent of the traders to claim most of the annuity for the debts owed them, but promised the Dakota he would not aid the merchants in this. Under this pressure from Sheehan, Galbraith released some food to the gathering.[29] Sheehan's handling of the situation was fair, but shortly afterward the Dakota would also witness how firm Sheehan could be.

Over the next few weeks, as soldiers, government officials, traders and the Dakota all waited for the arrival of the annuities, the volunteers amiably interacted with the Indians. Soldiers attended Dakota dances and distributed crackers or hardtack and water as Galbraith counted the Dakota families in anticipation of the impending payment. But these good relations soured when the Dakota decided to challenge the officials at the agency. Having patiently waited months for their money while their families slowly starved, the warriors decided it was time to take the food stored in the warehouses. They showed little concern over how the soldiers might react. The Dakota did not feel threatened by the military abilities of the handful of soldiers at the agency. They may also have felt that the accommodating Sheehan, a possible ally against the agent and traders, would not intervene. On August 4, between 400 and 800 warriors rushed the warehouses, broke in, and began carrying off numerous sacks of flour. Meanwhile, several hundred other warriors surrounded Sheehan and the soldiers guarding the buildings, stopping them from interfering.[30]

Encircled by hundreds of determined men, Sheehan, whose "face looked like a dead man's," ordered two howitzers aimed at the warehouse doors. In a commanding voice, Sheehan demanded the Dakota leave the buildings or he "would blow them to hell in less than a minute." Sheehan instructed Sgt. S. A. Trescott and sixteen men to drive the warriors out of the warehouses. It was a tense moment as Trescott and his men began to push their way through the crowd. Both sides pushed and shoved. Several fist fights broke out, and one private, knocked to the ground, was nearly scalped. Gradually, reluctantly, the Dakota retired from the buildings.[31] The Sioux were not looking for a violent confrontation. They had assumed the volunteers would not respond or could be intimidated into inaction; this was a mistake. Sheehan had responded firmly, but he had not overreacted. In using restraint, he avoided a bloody battle. Sheehan's actions were not typical of most Civil War volunteer officers, who usually responded with violence in similar situations involving Indians.

Relieved that his actions at the warehouse had been successful, Sheehan fumed over the fact that no agency official had come to the support of the army during the affair. Realizing that hunger would drive the Dakota to try again to take the warehouses, Sheehan pleaded with Galbraith to release the provisions. Galbraith adamantly refused, which made Sheehan even more frustrated with the narrow-minded agent. The lieutenant responded by writing Marsh. Sheehan explained the situation at the agency and urged Marsh to personally take charge there. Marsh agreed, arriving at the Upper Sioux Agency on August 6.[32]

Marsh reached the agency just as relations between the Dakota and the traders worsened. On August 5 and 6, Galbraith held meetings between Dakota leaders, Sheehan, and the traders. Galbraith hoped to persuade the traders to provide the Sioux with food on credit from their stores. In a heartless response, Andrew J. Myrick, a trader at the agency, replied to Galbraith's request by saying, "So far as I am concerned, if they are hungry, let them eat grass." When this was interpreted to the Dakota leaders, they were furious. Informed by Sheehan of what transpired at the meetings, Marsh immediately took action. Declaring that the distribution of food was now a military concern, he ordered Galbraith to release the supplies stored in the warehouses. One hundred and thirty barrels of flour and thirty barrels of pork were finally given to the hungry people. Soon after, most of the Dakota dispersed, intending to return when the annuity payment finally arrived. The crisis was over.[33]

The volunteers performed their duties admirably at the Upper Sioux Agency. Lieutenant Sheehan showed a clear understanding of the causes for the crisis and tried to keep the peace as impartially as he could in a difficult situation. He put pressure on Galbraith to release the food to the Dakota; yet, when warriors attempted to seize the supplies, Sheehan forced them to back down. Captain Marsh also acted wisely, providing the solution to the standoff. Although Galbraith, the traders, and the Dakota had all tried to manipulate the army, the volunteers continued to steer a neutral course; they refused to be controlled and followed the firm but fair policy of the prewar Regular Army.

Sadly, the efforts of the Minnesota volunteers to avoid a war with the Dakota failed. On August 17, after stealing some eggs, four young Sioux men killed five settlers near Acton, Minnesota. When news of the slayings reached the villages of the Mdewakanton and Wahpekute Dakota, it set off an uprising. The Dakota—oppressed, starving and angry—had had enough. They attacked the Lower Sioux Agency and killed the white civilians there, including the despised Andrew J. Myrick. Soon, Dakota war parties spread out across the Minnesota prairies, attacking unsuspecting settlers.[34]

Captain Marsh had demonstrated restraint and good judgment at the Upper Sioux Agency. However, when he received reports of the attack on the Lower Sioux Agency, he made a series of fatal mistakes. Marsh felt confident that a firm show of force would again restore order. He left Fort Ridgely, bound for the agency once more, ill-prepared to deal with the severity of the new situation. When informed by refugees of the extent of the uprising, he continued on. Overconfident, he led his men into an ambush at Redwood Ferry on the Minnesota River.

Tall grass grew on both sides of the road as it descended to the broad, wide river bottom where the ferry operated. Trees lined both banks. Marsh found the ferry owner's house vacant and the ferry boat unattended on the north side of the stream. The soldiers were preparing to cross the river when a Dakota named White Dog appeared on the west bank and shouted for the soldiers to cross. Marsh hesitated, fearing an ambush. Sergeant John Bishop reported spotting horses and men in the tall grass surrounding the column. His news was immediately followed by a devastating volley of gunfire from warriors hidden in the grass. Interpreter Peter Quinn, hit by over twenty bullets, fell dead along with at least twelve soldiers and Marsh's mule. The soldiers returned fire, and Marsh ordered a retreat to the nearby house, only to find it occupied by the Dakota. Completely surrounded, Marsh started a fighting withdrawal southward along the tree-covered north bank of the river. For four hours, the volunteers fought off attacks by their pursuers as they made their way downstream.[35]

Desperate to find a way to keep from being trapped, Marsh tried to ford the river, hoping to lead his battered command back to safety via the south bank. Marsh stumbled and drowned halfway across. The remaining soldiers scattered into tall grass along the shore. Sergeant Bishop rallied some of the men and led them back to the fort. Behind them, Marsh, Quinn, and twenty-two enlisted men lay dead.[36] With them died the volunteers' efforts to avoid war.

The Dakota War of 1862 left hundreds of slain on both sides. In the end the Santee were either driven into the Dakota Territory, where military expeditions in 1863 and 1864 continued to track down them and their Lakota relations, or banished from Minnesota to a new reservation near Fort Randall on the Missouri River. The Minnesota troops became much more belligerent towards

Indians. Lieutenant Gere, who had once played with Dakota children, wrote, "may the foul friends . . . be driven from the face of the earth." The aggressive attitude typical of other volunteers serving on the frontier became obvious among the Minnesota soldiers.[37] The battles and campaigns the Minnesota volunteers fought against the Dakota after the Redwood Ferry ambush were very much like those between other volunteers and tribes in the West. The volunteers in Minnesota were not responsible for starting the conflict, but in the end the Dakota War of 1862 was as brutal and as full of atrocities as those wars advocated and promoted by more aggressive soldiers fighting in the West.

Yet, prior to the outbreak of war in August 1862, the Minnesota volunteers had not pursued a harsh or violent policy towards Indians. Historians list numerous reasons for the Dakota War of 1862, including starvation, the injustice of the treaties and the annuities system, the forcible assimilation policies of the Indians, and the encroachments of whites settlers, but they never blame the army for the conflict. Adhering to the "firm but fair" policy of the regular army, the Minnesota volunteers prevented rather than provoked armed conflict. In their approach, the Minnesota volunteers stood out in sharp contrast to troops stationed near the Navajo and Apache or such Plains tribes as the Cheyenne and Arapaho.

Why the Minnesota volunteers were more restrained in their dealings with Indians is a question not easily answered. Minnesota was still considered a frontier region, like most areas of the West in which aggressive treatment of the Indians was the rule. At the start of the Civil War, the departure of Regular troops led to heightened fears of Indian attacks among settlers in Minnesota, just as it did other frontier whites. Minnesota soldiers, like other Western volunteers, believed Indians to be inferior and savage.

Perhaps the reason why the Minnesota soldiers treated Indians differently than other Westerners was because of the state's unique development. By the time Minnesota became a state in 1858 it was already quickly becoming a settled region. Over 150,000 whites lived there by that year, outnumbering the 8,000 Dakota by close to twenty-to-one. Settlers may have been concerned when regular soldiers left for the East, but there seemed to be no chance that the Dakota would or could seriously challenge white control of the state. The complete surprise with which so many settlers were taken indicated how few whites imagined that such a destructive war with the Dakota could occur. Finally, the Dakota were confined on a reservation. The Santee were virtually surrounded by settlers and were watched over by a fort located close by. In contrast, in some other Western states and territories large numbers of Indians still lived independently, surrounding and potentially threatening the smaller populations of whites. Given their dominance over the area, it is understandable why the Minnesota volunteers could accept and adopt the firm but fair policy of the Regulars. Officers such as Captain Marsh, believing that policy would prevent any serious hostilities, failed to see how close to war the Dakota were.[38]

NOTES

1. Isaac V. D. Heard, *History of the Sioux War and Massacres of 1862 and 1863* (New York: Harper and Brothers, 1865), 71-72; Board of Commissioners, compilers, *Minnesota in the Civil War and Indian Wars*, vol. 2 (St. Paul: Pioneer Press Co., 1899), 178; Lucy Leavenworth Wilder Morris, *Old Rail Fence Corners: Frontier Tales Told by Minnesota Pioneers* (St. Paul: Minnesota Historical Press, 1976), 146.

2. Thomas Gere, "A Scrap of Frontier History—Fort Ridgely," 8, manuscript collection, Minnesota Historical Society; Benjamin Randall, "The Siege of Fort Ridgely," manuscript collection, Minnesota Historical Society.

3. Gere, "A Scrap of Frontier History," 8; Benjamin Randall, *A Brief Sketch and History of Fort Ridgely* (Fairfax, MN: Fairfax Crescent Print, 1896), 6; Heard, *History of the Sioux War*, 71-72.

4. Alvin M. Josephy, Jr., *The Civil War in the American West* (New York: Alfred A. Knopf, 1991), xiii.

5. Francis Paul Prucha, *The Great Father: The United States Government and the American Indians* (Lincoln: University of Nebraska Press, 1984), 99; Francis Paul Prucha, *The Sword of the Republic* (Lincoln: University of Nebraska Press, 1969), xvi; Brad Agnew, *Fort Gibson: Terminal on the Trail of Tears* (Norman: University of Oklahoma Press, 1980), 6.

6. Robert M. Utley, *Frontiersmen in Blue: The United States Army and the Indians, 1848-1865* (Lincoln: University of Nebraska Press, 1967), 216-217; Josephy, *The Civil War in the American West*, xiii; Duane Schultz, *Month of the Freezing Moon: The Sand Creek Massacre, November 1864* (New York: St. Martin's Press, 1990), 51; T. R. Fehrenbach, *Comanche: The Destruction of a People* (New York: Alfred A. Knopf, 1983), 448, 460.

7. Edmond Jefferson Danziger, Jr., *Indians and Bureaucrats* (Urbana: University of Illinois Press, 1974), 98-99; Thomas Hughes, "The Treaty of Traverse des Sioux in 1851," *Minnesota Collections* vol. 10, part I (1900-1904, 1905), 106, 112; David A. Nichols, *Lincoln and the Indians: Civil War Policy and Politics* (Columbia: University of Missouri Press, 1978), 76.

8. Gary Clayton Anderson, *Kinsmen of Another Kind* (Lincoln: University of Nebraska Press, 1984), 4, 7-8; Roy W. Meyer, *History of the Santee Sioux* (Lincoln: University of Nebraska Press, 1967), 5-7, 21-22.

9. Fort Ridgely file, Miscellaneous Records, National Archives Record Group (NARG) 393, [United States] National Archives; Office of the U.S. Army Surgeon General, *Report of Sickness and Mortality in the Army of the United States*, vol. 2 (Washington, D. C.: A. O. P. Nicholson Printer, 1839-1855, 1956), 69; Sherry L. Smith, *The View from Officers' Row: Army Perceptions of Western Indians* (Tucson: University of Arizona Press, 1990), 95-98.

10. David A. Nichols, *Lincoln and the Indians*, 8-18, 65; Meyer, *History of the Santee*, 92, 105; Utley, *Frontiersmen in Blue*, 264.

11. Order no. 127, November 2, 1856, "Fort Ridgely Post Order Book," Minnesota Historical Society; Robert Murphy to Colonel E. B. Alexander, August 23, 1856, Fort Ridgely, Miscellaneous Documents, Minnesota Historical Society; Anderson, *Kinsmen of Another Kind*, 219, 228-229; Captain Sully to Lieutenant Hunter, August 6, 1857, Fort Ridgely, LS, NARG 393; Colonel Abercrombie to Assistant Adjutant General, June 24, 1858; Fort Ridgely, LR, NARG 393.

12. Fort Ridgely file, Miscellaneous Records, NARG 393; Gary Clayton Anderson, *Little Crow: Spokesman for the Sioux* (St. Paul: Minnesota Historical Society Press, 1986), 110-111; *Mankato Weekly Independent*, June 4, 1859; Special Order no. 12, February 28, 1860, "Fort Ridgely Post Order Book," Minnesota Historical Society; Major W. W. Morris to Assistant Adjutant General, March 7, 1860, Fort Ridgely, LS, NARG 393.

13. Anderson, *Kinsmen of Another Kind*, 207-208; Utley, *Frontiersmen in Blue*, 10; Colonel Abercrombie to Assistant Adjutant General, June 24, 1858, Fort Ridgely, LS, NARG 303; Major Day to Assistant Adjutant General, January 26, 1855, Fort Ridgely, LS, NARG 393.

14. Colonel Alexander to Agent Robert Murphy, August 13, 1856, Fort Ridgely, LS, NARG 393; Colonel Abercrombie to Commissioner of Indian Affairs, February 17, 1859; Fort Ridgely, LS, NARG 393; Paul N. Beck, "Fort Ridgely and the Settlement of the Minnesota River Valley, 1853-1867" (Ph.D. diss., Marquette University, 1996), 89-90.

15. *Mankato Weekly Independent*, May 6, 1861.

16. Thomas Patrick Gere, "Journal, 1861-1865," manuscript collection, Minnesota Historical Society; *Mankato Weekly Record*, June 28, 1861.

17. Alonzo L. Brown, *History of the Fourth Regiment of Minnesota Infantry Volunteers During the Great Rebellion* (St. Paul: Pioneer Press Company, 1892), 23-24; William Watts Folwell, *A History of Minnesota*, vol. 3 (St. Paul: Minnesota Historical Society, 1961), 81; Adjutant General of Minnesota, "Annual Report, 1861," manuscript collection, Minnesota Historical Society; Timothy J. Sheehan, "Diary, 1862," manuscript collection, Minnesota Historical Society.

18. Heard, *History of the Sioux War*, 71-72; Morris, *Old Rail Fence Corners*, 178; Sheehan, "Diary," July 19, July 26, 1862; Folwell, *A History of Minnesota*, vol. 2, 234.

19. Utley, *Frontiersmen in Blue*, 223; Clifford E. Trafzer, *The Kit Carson Campaign, the Last Great Navajo War* (Norman: University of Oklahoma Press, 1982), 67-69; C. L. Sonnichsen, *The Mescalero Apaches* (Norman: University of Oklahoma Press, 1971), 110.

20. Indian Agent Thomas Falbraith to Captain A. K. Skano, September 14, 1861, Fort Ridgely, LR, NARG 393; Thomas Galbraith to Superintendent W. Thompson, October 1, 1861, in Commissioner of Indian Affairs, *Annual Report*; *Mankato Semi-Weekly Record*, August 27, September 10, 1861; Thomas Galbraith to Captain L. L. Baxter, December 25, 1862, Fort Ridgely, LR, NARG 393.

21. Duane Schultz, *Over the Earth I Come: The Great Sioux Uprising of 1862* (New York: St. Martin's Press, 1992), 11; Myer, *History of the Santee*, 109; Sheehan, "Diary," September 7, 1862.

22. Kenneth Carley, *The Sioux Uprising of 1862* (St. Paul: Minnesota Historical Society Press, 1961), 3-4; Schultz, *Over the Earth I Come*, 6, 8-9.

23. Schultz, *Over the Earth I Come*, 5.

24. Anderson, *Little Crow*, 121-122.

25. Charles S. Bryant and Abel B. Murch, *A History of the Great Massacre by the Sioux Indians in Minnesota* (Cincinnati: Rickey and Carroll, Publishers, 1864), 86-187.

26. Anderson, *Little Crow*, 122; Gere, "Journal," April 16, 1862; Bryant and Murch, *History of the Great Massacre*, 186-187.

27. Anderson, *Little Crow*, 122; Schultz, *Over the Earth I Come*, 11-12; Board of Commissioners, *Minnesota in the Civil War and the Indian Wars*, vol. 2, 163-164.

28. Gere, "Journal," March 9, June 30, 1862; Board of Commissioners, *Minnesota in the Civil War and the Indian Wars*, vol. 2, 163-164.

29. Anderson, *Little Crow*, 123; Sheehan, "Diary," July 8, 1862.

30. Sheehan, "Diary," July 13, July 22, July 26, 1862; Board of Commissioners, *Minnesota in the Civil War and the Indian Wars*, vol. 2, 176-177; Anderson, *Kinsmen of Another Kind*, 250.

31. Anderson, *Kinsmen of Another Kind*, 250; Sheehan, "Diary," August 4, August 6, 1862; Orlando McFall, "Narrative of the Sioux Indian Massacre in 1862," 5-10, manuscript collection, Minnesota Historical Society.

32. Sheehan, "Diary," August 6, 1862; Anderson, *Little Crow*, 124; Meyer, *History of the Santee*, 112.

33. Sheehan, "Diary," August 6, 1862; Schultz, *Over the Earth I Come*, 26-28; McFall, "Narrative of the Indian Massacre of 1862," 15-16; Board of Commissioners, *Minnesota in the Civil War and the Indian Wars*, vol. 2, 178.

34. Utley, *Frontiersmen in Blue*, 264.

35. Folwell, *History of Minnesota*, vol. 2, 112-114; Board of Commissioners, *Minnesota in the Civil War and the Indian Wars*, vol. 2, 167-169, 179-180; Heard, *History of the Sioux War*, 73.

36. Board of Commissioners, *Minnesota in the Civil War and the Indian Wars*, vol. 2, 167-181, 179-180; Schultz, *Over the Earth I Come*, 58.

37. Danziger, Jr., *Indians and Bureaucrats*, 109; Meyer, *History of the Sioux*, 124, 142; Gere, "Journal," November, 1862; *St. Paul Pioneer and Democrat*, September 4, 1862.

38. Meyer, *History of the Santee*, 115; Carley, *The Sioux Uprising of 1862*, 218; Schultz, *Over the Earth I Come*, 5; Utley, *Frontiersmen in Blue*, 262-264.

OUTSTANDING NEW BOOKS FOR SPRING 2000!

Breaking the Backbone of the Rebellion: The Final Battles of the Petersburg Campaign
A. Wilson Greene

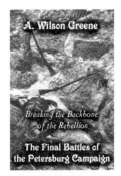

The first full-length study of the final assaults against Lee's lines below Petersburg and the dramatic fall of that city and Richmond. This detailed and outstanding battle history is jammed with photos. Maps by George Skoch, Foreword by Richard Sommers. Greene is the director of Pamplin Park Historic Site, the scene of the subject of much of this book. ISBN: 1-882810-48-1. 576pp. Cloth. $34.95

April 2000

The Civil War in Kentucky: Battle in the Bluegrass State
Kent Masterson Brown

The **best** book on the Kentucky war, written by leading scholars in the field. Authors include John Y. Simon, Charles Roland, Lowell Harrison, Wiley Sword, James Ramage, Kent M. Brown, and others. Topics include battles of Munfordville, Mill Springs, Perryville, Richnond, Morgan's Raid, Pat Cleburne, the Orphan Brigade, Confederate defense of Kentucky, and more. ISBN 1-882810-47-3. 360pp., maps, photos. Cloth. $29.95

May 2000

Lost for the Cause: The Confederate Army in 1864
Steven H. Newton

An original and rigorously researched study on the numbers and units available to the Confederacy in the pivotal year of 1864. Newton has discovered that the South had large numbers of men available it did not know it had in scores of misplaced units, which resulted in squandered opportunities. His conclusions rewrite the history of the war's most decisive year. ISBN: 1-882810-49-X. 336pp. Cloth. $29.95

June 2000

Savas Publishing Company

202 First Street SE, Suite 103A, Mason City, IA 50401; 515-421-7135 (phone); 515-421-8370 (fax); cwbooks@mach3ww.com (e-mail); www.savaspublishing.com (website)

"The most terrible stories"

THE 1862 DAKOTA CONFLICT
IN WHITE IMAGINATION

Ellen Farrell

On August 27, 1862, the *Faribault* [Minnesota] *Central Republican* wrote, "Little did we dream that almost in our very midst was a slumbering volcano, ready at any moment to burst forth." This expression of surprise and anger came in response to news that, ten days earlier, Dakota Indians had attacked the Lower Sioux (Redwood) Agency, less than a hundred miles from Faribault. Since then, the Indians had been raiding cabins in the area of the agency and killing white settlers, apparently indiscriminately. "Yet such it seems is too true," the report continued, "and now, we turn to find ourselves plunged into the horrors of a savage struggle. . . . Men, women, and children, peaceably pursuing their daily avocations, have been cruelly and inhumanly mangled and murdered by these fiends in human shape."[1]

Throughout the Dakota War of 1862, rhetoric like that of the *Central Republican* pervaded the reports of the Minnesota press and the outcries of Minnesota citizens. Two assumptions dominated all white discussions of events. The first was that the attacks represented an act of Indian unity. The so-called "Sioux Uprising" was seen as a massive undertaking by all Sioux-speaking nations and perhaps by other Indian peoples as well. According to the *Central Republican* newspaper, "There seems to have been a general and preconcerted uprising of all the tribes of the Sioux and it is feared that the Chippeways [sic] and other powerful tribes are also united with them in their bloody work of carnage and death."[2] The second supposition was that the Dakota were uniformly and without exception guilty of unprovoked atrocities.

In the words of Faribault's journalists, the conflict was "a savage struggle with the inhuman barbarians that have wrongfully been permitted to occupy a large portion of the most beautiful sections of our State."[3]

These two misperceptions persisted in popular imagination and, if sometimes more subtly, in histories written about the conflict.[4] The complexities which existed in Dakota society and in the interaction of white and Indian cultures were ignored and even deliberately obscured.

The Dakota were seen as "inhuman barbarians . . . [and] fiends in human shape" who were unified in hostility.[5] This dehumanization of the Indians was in part the result of terror and anger. But the assumptions were also, in perhaps an unselfconscious but quite self-serving way, a means of defending the racism and land hunger of white Minnesotans. If the war was a premeditated crime by the Sioux as a whole, all of the spurious treaties, subverted annuity payments, and demands for reservation takeovers in Minnesota could be justified.

In reality, the beginning of the war in Minnesota took many Sioux by surprise. The Indians entered the conflict only after being driven to "a starving condition and desperate state of mind."[6] The Dakota nation committed itself to war without consensus, and the conflict served to divide them further. Many, probably a majority, of the Dakota did not participate in the hostilities, and many of those who did participate harbored considerable ambivalence towards their actions.[7] Even the popular name of the war, the "Minnesota Sioux War," is misleading, for only some of the subdivisions of the Dakota or Santee nation of the Sioux were involved, and the uninvolved Nakota and Teton (Lakota) nations were not residents of Minnesota.

The Dakota conflict began in a small enough way, certainly small enough to belie the *Central Republican*'s notion that hostilities had begun as "a general and preconcerted uprising of all the tribes of the Sioux." On Sunday morning, August 17, 1862, four young Dakotas (Brown Wing, Killing Ghost, Breaking Up, and Runs Against Something Crawling) were hunting near Acton, Minnesota. Their hunt had been unsuccessful, and they were discouraged and thirsty as they came upon the farm of Robinson Jones. After speaking with the four men a moment, Jones dismissed them and went to a neighbor's house. The four young men followed and proceeded to challenge Jones and another white man to a friendly game of target practice. This sort of interaction was nothing unusual. Indeed, on the frontier white settlers and Dakota often socialized and even helped each other in times of need. Once all had participated in the shooting contest, the four young braves casually reloaded their weapons and,

Little Crow

National Archives

"without warning . . . in apparent retaliation for an insult," fired upon the whites present, killing three men and a woman.[8] On their way off the property, they shot and killed a fourteen-year-old girl who was probably standing in the doorway of a cabin.

The four attackers hurried back to their village, Rice Creek, to report what they had done and to summon support. Early the next morning, a large group of warriors approached Little Crow, an influential leader of the Mdewakanton bands of Dakota. Most of the men were bent on war, but some of the older ones appealed to Little Crow not to act rashly. "You are about to commit an act like that of the porcupine, who climbs a tree, balances himself upon a springy bough, and then gnaws off the very bough upon which he is sitting," the elderly Tamahay told the assembled group. "[To fight] is self-destruction."[9]

Little Crow was pulled in opposing directions by the dissenting voices present. Finally, frustrated by the chief's hesitation, one of the war advocates "brazenly accused him of cowardice."[10] Little Crow responded furiously and eloquently. The Mdewakanton leader knew that instigating a conflict with whites was foolish, but the charge of faintheartedness rankled him. His inner conflict—parallel to the division which existed among the Dakota over whether to commit to war—was apparent in his mix of militancy and caution: "Ta-o-ya-te-du-ta [Little Crow] is not a coward, and he is not a fool!" Yet he then scolded the warriors for being foolish, "like little children," and warned them that picking a fight with the whites would be imprudent indeed. Little Crow expanded his argument: "We are only little herds of buffaloes left scattered. . . . Kill one—two—ten [of the whites], and ten times ten will come to kill you. Count your fingers all day long and white men with guns in their hands will come faster than you can count. . . ."

Yet, after thoroughly outlining the many reasons not to escalate the conflict, Little Crow expressed a surprising decision as he made one last reproach of the warriors' folly. "You will die like the rabbits when the hungry wolves hunt them in the Hard Moon," he portended. Yet, he concluded, "Ta-o-ya-te-du ta is not a coward: he will die with you."[11] Despite his realization of the foolishness of such an undertaking, Little Crow chose to join the angry warriors in a fight to preserve their old way of life. The result would be a six-week conflict resulting in the deaths of about 500 whites and an even greater number of Dakota Sioux.[12]

The divisions among the men at the war council—and in all of Dakota society—were the result of sweeping white settlement of Dakota lands. By 1862, settlers had made deep inroads west into Minnesota, taking over territory that had once been the domain and means of livelihood of these seasonally migratory Indians. Settlers established farms, railroads, towns and industries, and, slowly, treaty by treaty, confined Indians to small reservations. The Treaty of Traverse des Sioux had been especially devastating; its "adjustment" by officials in Washington had left the Dakotas only a strip of land along the Minnesota River.[13] On its confines, politically appointed and often inept Indian agents presided, and residents were given insufficient annuities with which to purchase supplies from often dishonest traders. Many Indians wished to live as they did before the treaties—going where they pleased and when they pleased, hunting game wherever they could find it, selling their furs to the traders and living off of natural resources.[14]

Indian agents and other whites who interacted with Indians on the reservation were fiercely dedicated to what they considered "civilizing" the Dakota. In the view of traditional Indians, this was arrogant and offensive. As one chief, Big Eagle, explained, Euro-Americans seemed "to say by their manner when they saw an Indian, 'I am much better than you,' and the Indians did not like this." He also observed that if the Indians had tried to make the whites live like them, the whites would have resisted in the same way the Indians did.[15]

The Minnesota treaties and the attempts by whites to impose their culture on the Indians also led to friction among the Dakota themselves. Indians who turned from a hunter-gatherer lifestyle to an agricultural way of life were rewarded. The Upper Sioux Agency and Lower Sioux Agency officials favored the most compliant Indians by building them brick homes and allotting them special supplies. This caused envy and dislike among other Dakotas, who called the recipients "farmers" as a form of disgrace. The traditionals retaliated by calling the converts "cut-hairs" or "breeches men," because they had given up the Indian fashion of long male hair and no longer wore breech clouts and blanket wrappings.[16]

Little Crow displayed a personal ambivalence towards assimilation that seemed to reflect the divisions within the Dakota nation. He had moved all four of his wives and seven of his ten children into a 2-story frame house (surrounding tipis supplied extra sleeping capacity) and declared he would try his hand at farming. To encourage this process, the Lower Sioux Agency agent promised to construct a brick house for Little Crow by the end of 1862. However, when Chief Wabasha traveled to Washington in 1858 bearing a letter insisting that the Dakota wanted to "leave off the war path" and adopt white ways if given land to do so, Little Crow had been one of the only two Dakotas leaders not to sign the letter.[17]

Hardships by mid-1862 heightened the tensions among the Dakotas and between the Indians and whites on the central Minnesota reservations. The summer of that year was particularly dismal for the Dakota. Delivery of supplies to the Lower or Redwood Agency was delayed. Compounding this problem was the Treasury Department, which "debated for a month whether to make the [treaty annuity] payments in gold or in greenbacks."[18] Indian agent Thomas Galbraith refused to issue needed provisions until the annuities came, in order to simplify distribution. Traders refused to extend additional credit to the Indians. On Friday, August 15, two days before the first killings at Acton, Little Crow confronted Galbraith: "We have waited a long time. The money is ours but we cannot get it. We have no food, but here are these stores, filled with food. We ask that you, the agent, make some arrangement by which we can get food from the stores, or else we may take our own way to keep ourselves from starving. When men are hungry they help themselves."[19]

Despite the shadow of threat in Little Crow's statement, Galbraith characterized the meeting as "friendly" and "believed he had completely secured that chief's good will and cooperation in the work of civilization. He 'understood' that the chief was ready to abandon the 'blanket Indians' and 'become a white man.'"[20] On Sunday, Little Crow "attended church there [at the Episcopal Mission at the agency] . . . listened closely to the sermon and [shook] hands with everybody," Big Eagle would later recall. Yet the next day, "Little

Crow was on the ground directing operations" in the Dakota's first substantial attack, against the same agency.[21]

While Little Crow represented a singular case of personal ambivalence, the mixed-blood people on the reservation were as a group even more representative of the divisions within Dakota society. These part-white, part-Dakota individuals comprised 15 percent of the Dakota reservation population in 1862.[22] Gabriel Renville, a half-white man who was raised as a Dakota, described the ambiguous status of the mixed-bloods by stating that, "though they were white, [they] were children of the Indians."[23] The outbreak of hostilities created a dilemma for all such persons of mixed ancestry.

Even before the war, many mixed-bloods had chosen to identify with white society, to the extent that when the conflict came, they viewed all unassimilated Indians as "horrifying."[24] Samuel J. Brown, son of a mixed-blood Dakota woman and a white Indian agent, went so far as to describe one so-called "hostile" Indian as "by far the ugliest looking and most repulsive specimen of humanity I had ever seen."[25] Cecilia Campbell Stay, a mixed-blood woman living at the Lower Sioux Agency when the conflict erupted, related that "through the day there were many Indians gathered in front of the house. . . . [Later] they left and bothered us no more with the sight of their unsightly hideousness."[26]

The outbreak of hostilities forced many mixed-bloods to take sides militarily as well as culturally. Nancy McClure Faribault Huggan, for example, was the child of a full-blood Dakota womon and a white lieutenant at Fort Snelling. In addition, she was married to a white trader, David Faribault, one of the few traders whom the Indians considered to be honest. Huggan's sentiments were clear: she was so pleased when an army expedition brought in artillery to deal with the outbreak that she declared "the sound of [expedition command Henry H.] Sibley's guns was as sweet [as] the chimes of wedding bells to the bride." Recalling her experiences later, Huggan said, "it did me real good to learn that so many of my race had stood loyal and true [to the whites] and had done such good service. You know that only a very few mixed-bloods took part in the outbreak."[27]

However, a few individuals of dual parentage did side with the Dakota combatants. One, George Quinn, explained his involvement in the following way: "I am half white man and half Indian, and I learned to read and write the Sioux language. . . . But I never learned to speak English and I was raised among the Indians as one of them. So when the outbreak came I went with my people against the whites. I was nineteen years old and anxious to distinguish myself in the war. . . ."[28] Still other mixed-bloods, when confronted with the reality of the hostilities, adopted a middle position and attempted to mediate the conflict. One example is that of Gabriel Renville. The child of two-mixed bloods, Renville had been raised as a Dakota after his widowed mother remarried a full-blood Dakota. Renville, who never learned to speak English, identified with the Dakotas and had never learned to speak English. Despite this, he opposed both sides' actions in the conflict because of the suffering they imposed upon women and children.

However, it was not simply mixed-blood individuals who found themselves with divided loyalties. The entire Dakota nation was split over the issue of war. The conflict not only brought divisions in full-blood Dakota society to the fore, but exacerbated them. Already at odds with one another over accommodation to whites prior to the conflict, the Dakota were also divided in their opinions on the war effort. Many Dakota, including several prominent chiefs, disapproved of the warriors' actions and were particularly disgusted by the killing of white women and children. The young braves who had instigated the conflict with the initial killings at Acton found themselves the subjects of hatred by some in their own community. According to Good Star Woman, "One of them was sitting at the end of his wigwam, opposite the door, when an Indian came in and said, 'You were the cause of much suffering, making the women and children suffer so much,' and he shot him dead. [Another] went out of his tent and was walking along when someone shot him in the back. One of the leaders said, 'This is what we ought to have done in the beginning and then this suffering would not have come.'"[29]

Even the Dakota committed to the fighting argued over the conduct of the war. Their nominal leader, Little Crow, at times vocally disapproved of the manner in which the warriors were waging war. In addition, several of the chiefs spent valuable hours in the early part of the hostilities arguing about strategy, when decisive action and unified purpose could have given them an early advantage.

A final indication of the deep divisions within Sioux society is the fact that the Dakota warriors ultimately blamed the opposition of the mixed-bloods and other "Christian" Indians, rather than the reaction of the whites, for their ultimate defeat. Little Crow summarized this attitude with his reaction after the Battle of Wood Lake on September 23, 1862, the first decisive defeat of the Dakota. "Despondent . . . [and] almost heartbroken," he told his people that he was "ashamed to call himself a Sioux." He continued: "To be sure, the whites had big guns and better arms than the Indians and outnumbered us four or five to one, but that is no reason we should not have whipped them, for we are brave men while they are cowardly women. I cannot account for the disgraceful defeat. It must be the work of traitors in our midst."[30]

Part of the defeated Dakotas' reaction was probably based on the fact that mixed-bloods had often warned white friends of the danger of impending attacks. A typical case was that of the Garrison family. According to observer Clara Janvier Kinkead, a "half-breed" family friend who had himself escaped from the warriors, warned the family of danger in time for them to escape to safety.[31] However, the full bloods went so far as to accuse the mixed-bloods of actively assisting the U.S. army. Nancy Faribault Huggan, who was held captive in a camp of "hostiles," described a significant scene as the warriors came in from their first decisive defeat on September 23: "Very soon stragglers came in bearing wounded, singing the death song and telling the tale of defeat. They were cursing the half-breeds, saying that [Col. Henry H.] Sibley had numbers of them with him in the battle [at Wood Lake, Minnesota], and that every shot that one of them fired had hit an Indian." Huggan reported as late as 1894 that "The Indians have always bitterly hated the half-breeds for their conduct in favor of whites . . . and they hate them still. It seems they can forgive everybody but us."[32]

The white assumption that the "Sioux" were unified in hostility was simply incorrect. So was the charge that all the Dakotas were "inhuman barbarians" who killed indiscriminately and irrationally at every opportunity. Some whites even maintained, in contradiction to the fiction of Indian unity, that the Dakota even massacred mixed-bloods and Indian peace advocates. It is true that some Dakotas, often identifiable individuals, did commit unspeakable atrocities upon white settlers. But the spontaneous negotiations that frequently occurred indicate that many combatants were discerning. In particular, many Dakota warriors—as many mixed-bloods and whites—were loath to harm old friends who had overnight been classed as enemies.

One example of such Dakota clemency is the case of Susan Frenier Brown, a woman of mixed ancestry who called upon her Dakota ancestry to save her white family and several settlers. Brown's family and neighbors were traveling by wagon to escape the hostilities when they were overtaken by a war party. Her son Samuel later recalled that his mother quickly "grasped the situation" and "knew that to save us she must speak and make herself known. . . . So she stood up in the wagon, and waving her shawl she cried in a loud voice that she was a Sisseton [division Dakota]—a relative of Waanatan, Scarlet Plume, Sweetcorn, Ah-Kee-Pah and the friend of Standing Buffalo, that she had come down this way for protection and hoped to get it." The warriors reacted dubiously, but one recognized Brown. She had saved his life by nursing him the winter before, and he insisted that none of her party be harmed. "The others withdrew sullenly, saying 'they would kill the white men, anyway.'" Brown, however, would not stand for that, and "after much bitter wrangling, and mainly through the persuasive eloquence of our friend, they reluctantly decided to accede to the wishes of my mother . . . and let them go."[33]

One unusual case of discrimination—one that involved two opponents of mixed ancestry—was that of George Quinn. Quinn, who chose to fight with the Dakota, was spared by an acquaintance. Sent with four other braves to scout out the white stronghold at Fort Ridgely, Quinn and his party arrived late at night, crawled up as close as they dared to the fort, and fell asleep. "When I awoke," Quinn recalled, "it was daybreak, and old Jack Frazer, a well-known half-breed who had made his escape from Wacouta's village the day before, leaving his family behind, was standing picket in plain view of us. He called out to us to get right away from there or he would shoot us, and he said that if he did not know our fathers and mothers so well he would shoot us anyhow."[34]

Also, despite threats to the contrary, Dakota warriors showed a decided reluctance to harm mixed-bloods or other of their communities who advocated peace. In one situation, Gabriel Renville and a group of peace advocates had formed a camp not far from a war camp. Renville decided to invite the warriors to discuss making peace. The peace camp prepared a large feast, but before the invitation could be issued to the other encampment, a large party of combatants approached on horseback. Renville recalled: "They all had their guns, their faces were painted, and they were gaily dressed. They came and stopped at our camp. Then I said to them, 'We were about to send for you to come here to a council. But as you are here, whatever your purpose may be in coming, for the present get off your horses and have something to eat.' They then got down, and after they had eaten they mounted again, and, forming around our camp, said, 'We have come for you, and if you do not come, the next time we will come to attack you;' and firing their guns into the air they departed."[35]

However, no such attack on the peaceful Dakotas ever took place. Renville recounted a second occasion when warriors approached and threatened his peaceful camp. A peace advocate called out to them, "If you come any nearer we will shoot. Why are you treating us this way? . . . Go back." The party responded by retreating without incident. A few days later, the peace camp had moved to new grazing lands. "There again the Medawakanton [the most militant division of the Dakota] soldiers came, and having taken us unawares pushed over some of our tents, but on being ordered to stop they quit and went back to their camp."[36] The hostile Indians seem never to have seriously intended seriously to harm the peace advocates; rather, they may have been trying merely to intimidate them from interfering with the war effort.

Not even the despised mixed-bloods were attacked by the war faction. Recognizing that the majority of those with dual ancestry sided with the whites or advocated peace, the hostile warriors often threatened to kill them en masse during the conflict. However, they did not follow through on these threats. Instead, existing ties often led to extraordinary negotiations over the lives of relatives and friends. For example, according to Nancy Faribault Huggan, one day at the camp where hostages were held, "the cry was raised that the half-breeds were all to be killed. Little Crow held a council and would allow no Indians to attend it that had half-breed relatives. We thought this looked bad for us. . . ." But then Huggan's full-blood uncle, Rattling Walker, came to the camp and declared he would take his relatives away with him. Little Crow and his soldiers raised a protest, but Rattling Walker simply said, "Little Crow, I only want the people who belong to me, and I will take them. You think you are brave because you have killed so many white people. You have surprised them; they were not prepared for you, and you know it. . . . Now, I am going to take my people, and I would like to see the man that will stop me!" Huggans and her family had started away from the camp with Rattling Walker when "some of the Indians raised the war whoop. But we kept on . . . Little Crow and his warriors looking sullenly but silently at us."[37]

All of these examples point to the fact that the Dakotas were not united and were not engaged in a wholly indiscriminate rampage. Furthermore, to hold the view that they were all "inhuman savages" required ignoring the fact that, before the conflict, whites and Indians had interacted on many levels and in many contexts. These dealings ranged from the transactions of the Indian agents, to efforts to encourage assimilation by well meaning whites, to interracial marriages that produced many mixed-blood offspring. Yet, misguided perceptions of the Dakotas lasted throughout and long after the conflict.

Why were the misconceptions about the Dakotas so widespread and persistent in white imagination? The first and most obvious reason is fear. To unprepared white settlers, the attacks seemed sudden, arbitrary, and overwhelming. The emotional impact was so great that white settlers of twenty-three Minnesota counties fled east in terror, "many of them carrying nothing but the clothes worn at the moment of escape. . . . Not a few left the state never to return. In all, a region 200 miles long and averaging 50 miles wide was devastated or depopulated [of whites]."[38]

A correspondent for the *St. Paul* [Minnesota] *Press* described the excitement—[and] general confusion" which reigned in the town of Monticello, a hundred miles from any fighting, six days after the killings began:

> The whole country [,] . . . an area forty by twenty miles, has been on the move since 6 o'clock yesterday evening. . . . The cause of this seems to have originated in the excited imagination of a poor frightened woman, who thought she saw savages skulking in the bushes near her house, and uttered those now fearful words, 'the Indians are coming!' The public mind had been prepared by recent outrages, and the excitement was most intense. . . . The families were all aroused, and the women and children taken to the hotel; men ran in every direction for guns, pitchforks, &c.; wagons kept coming, but nobody could be found who had seen an Indian."[39]

The power of fearful imagination is also evident in the story of Clara Janvier Kinkead, one of the first settlers of the central lakes region of Minnesota. Though Clara's husband initially kept the extent of the danger from her, he eventually recommended that she go with the children to the home of neighbors, the Shotwells. Clara got ready in half an hour, gathering only a few items, as she "fully expected to be back in a few days." Shortly, a wagon caravan made up of neighbors who were "almost frightened to death" passed by the Shotwells' house, imploring the Kinkeads to join them. Clara's husband believed that these travelers were exaggerating the proximity of the menace and wanted to stay. The next day, exhausted soldiers arrived at the house and explained to the settlers the growing extent of the hostilities. The troops reported that they had barely escaped with their lives from what was becoming a storm center down south. At nine o'clock that night, the Kinkeads and the Shotwells set off again. "Such a night," wrote Clara, "I hope never to spend again. We expected every minute to be surrounded and killed by the Indians."[40]

Within a few miles traveling after daybreak, the Kinkeads caught up to their neighbors, who had been joined by other fleeing whites. From the head of the wagon train, Clara "looked back and counted sixty white covered wagons following us. We were flying for our lives in ox-teams. . . ." The entire journey of about sixty miles to St. Cloud, Minnesota, took the train about a week. During this time, said Clara, "We saw no Indians, but as other families would join our train, we would hear most awful accounts of murders and captures, from about five miles from where we were. . . . Oh, the most terrible stories! Enough to set us almost frantic!"[41] The wagon train passed through several towns that were virtually deserted. The refugees' destination, St. Cloud, was so crowded that there were no lodgings or provisions available for people or livestock. The Kinkeads and their neighbors cannot be blamed for wanting to escape the real and violent end that had come to many settlers near the Minnesota River reservations. But at no time had the Kinkeads or their neighbors actually ever seen such violence by Indians; they were driven solely by the terrorizing reports and rumors of others.

The fear held by white Minnesotans mixed with a second factor, racial prejudice, to create the common misconceptions about the Dakotas. The racism of the nineteenth century arose out of a widely held set of ideas regarding the inferiority and barbarism of American Indians. These concepts were not only popular, but were even supported by supposed intellectuals. By 1862, the U.S. government already had a long history of westward "Indian Removal." Many whites wanted the Indians, already forced west of the Mississippi River, to be pushed beyond the organized states and territories west of the river. Various theorists went to great lengths to justify the rights of whites to remove Indians from desirable land on specious "scientific" grounds. Many declared that the various races were unequal, some even stating that certain races had actually been created separately as distinct species. Physician and phrenologist Samuel G. Morton, for example, argued that God had given the white race "a decided and unquestioned superiority over all the nations of the earth." In 1842, Morton had written, "Was it not for [white] mental superiority, these happy climes which we now inhabit would yet be possessed by the wild and untutored Indian, and that soil which now rejoices the hearts of millions of freemen, would be yet overrun by lawless tribes of contending barbarism."[42]

Such "scientific" justifications for Indian removal inspired a suspicion in whites that no matter how "civilized" the Indians might appear, lurking just below the surface was a "wild[,] unearthly[,] . . . savage passion," something altogether "inhuman." White fears that the Dakota conflict was an evolutionary battle between civilization and savagery inspired statements like the *Faribault*

A fanciful depiction of the largest mass execution in United States History.
Thirty-eight Sioux were hanged at Fort Mankato, Minnesota following the
collapse of the 1862 Dakota Uprising. *National Archives*

Central Republican's appeal to "drive [the Indians] far beyond our borders, that
peace and security may once more reign."[43] During and after the Dakota war,
demands to drive the Indians further westward were partially inspired by the
desire for security, as the *Central Republican*'s remark suggests. However,
such demands suggest a third reason for popular misconceptions about the
conflict—the need to justify past and future expropriations of Indian land in
Minnesota. The conflict gave whites the excuse to do what they had been
tempted to do since they first decided that Dakota was desirable: demonize the
Sioux entirely and remove them.

As the Dakota war effort collapsed, anger, prejudice, and the popular
misunderstandings of the conflict led to white calls for extermination, revenge,
and land seizures. The *Central Republican* demanded, as an alternative to
driving the Indians west, that white Minnesotans "wipe out the treacherous,
accursed vipers."[44] The U.S. Army proceeded to do just that judicially.
Following the hostilities, a military commission put several hundred Dakota on
trial for their actions. General John Pope, exiled to Minnesota following his
disastrous defeat at Second Bull Run in August 1862, directed Col. Henry
Sibley not to hesitate to execute any Sioux who were found innocent of taking
part in the hostilities. However, explained Pope, "It is my purpose utterly to
exterminate the Sioux. They are to be treated as maniacs or wild beasts."

Colonel Sibley, in turn, maintained that "necessity must be my justification [for the] forthwith" execution of what would turn out to be 303 Dakotas condemned to death.[45] These officers' actions were in line with what the *Central Republican* had hoped early in the conflict: that the conflict would be a "war of extermination."[46]

The desire of the writers of the *Central Republican* and the white population of Minnesota for revenge were not fully appeased by what would be the largest mass execution in U.S. history. President Lincoln, disturbed by the haste and passion with which the Indians had been sentenced, examined the trial records. In an act of significant political courage, Lincoln commuted all but thirty-eight sentences on the grounds that only rapists and murderers, and not legitimate combatants, should be executed.[47] The sentence was carried out at a mass hanging in Mankato on December 27, 1862. The *Central Republican* reported on the event with satisfaction. "As the [gallows'] drop fell the citizens could not repress a shout of exultation, and the soldiers joined. A boy soldier, who stood beside me, had his mother, and brothers and sisters, killed [by the Indians]; his face was pale and quivering, but he gave a shout of righteous exultation when the drop fell."[48]

Those Dakotas who were not imprisoned or killed were forced to flee to the Dakota Territory [the current states of North and South Dakota] or Canada. All Dakota land in Minnesota was seized without compensation by the governor, and treaties with the Dakota nation were abrogated. Anti-Indian sentiment remained high among white Minnesotans well into the twentieth century. Nor were just the Dakota affected. In 1863 and 1864, the army launched what were regarded in part as punitive expeditions against the Dakotas who had fled into Dakota Territory. In the process, the United States drew the previously uninvolved Nakota and Lakota peoples into what would be a twenty-seven year conflict with those other "Sioux" nations.

Though some Dakota were indeed guilty of killings and atrocities, white imagination inflated a racially based assumption of Indian savagery until all Minnesota Indians were seen as monolithically united in barbarism. This perception was held despite the fact that the aggression had been initiated and carried out by a minority of the Dakotas, and then only when provoked. In a self-serving fashion, this perception was utilized as an excuse to remove the Dakotas out of Minnesota entirely. Poignantly, Little Crow expressed his understanding of this injustice in a mid-conflict letter of negotiation to his old hunting companion Sibley. Little Crow asserted simply, "It ain't all our fault."[49]

NOTES

1. Peg Meier, *Coffee Made Her Insane, and Other Nuggets from Old Minnesota Newspapers* (Minneapolis, MN: Neighbors, 1988), 57.

2. Ibid.

3. The conflict was long referred to as "The Great Sioux Uprising" by white authors. See, for example, C. M. Oehler, *The Great Sioux Uprising* (New York: Oxford University Press, 1959). Meier, *Coffee Made Her Insane*, 57.

4. A good example of the racial attitudes and assumptions of contemporary white historians is that of Isaac V. D. Heard, *History of the Sioux War and Massacres of 1862 and 1863* (New York: Harper & Brothers, 1865). Heard opens his chapter on causes of the war by stating: "The Indians were predisposed to hostility toward the whites. They regarded them with that repugnance which God has implanted as an instinct in different races for the preservation of their national integrity, and to prevent the subjection of the inferior in industry and intelligence to the superior." Ibid., 31.

5. *Faribault* [Minn.] *Central Republican*, August 27, 1862, in Meier, *Newspapers*, 58.

6. Robert Hakewaste's Testimony, in Gary Clayton Anderson and Alan R. Woolworth, eds., *Through Dakota Eyes* (St. Paul: Minnesota Sate Historical Society, 1988), 32.

7. For example, Big Eagle, reported that "when the [Dakota] force started down to attack the [Lower Sioux] agency [on August 18, the first day of the conflict], I went along. I did not lead my band, and I took no part in the killing. I went to save the lives of two particular friends if I could. I think others went for the same reason, for nearly every Indian had a friend that he did not want killed;" Big Eagle's Account, in Anderson and Woolworth, eds., *Through Dakota Eyes*, 56.

8. William Watts Folwell, *A History of Minnesota*, vol. 2 (St. Paul, MN: Minnesota Historical Society, 1924), 417.

9. Duane Schultz, *Over the Earth I Come* (New York: St. Martin's Press, 1992), 41.

10. Little Crow's Speech, in Anderson and Woolworth, eds., *Through Dakota Eyes*, 40.

11. Little Crow's Speech, in Anderson and Woolworth, eds., *Through Dakota Eyes*, 40-42.

12. Meier, *Newspapers*, 57.

13. The treaties of Traverse des Sioux and Mendota (1851) ceded about twenty-four million acres of Sioux land to whites; Theodore C. Blegen, *Minnesota: A History of the State* (St. Paul, Minnesota: University of Minnesota, 1975), 167

14. Big Eagle's Account, in Anderson and Woolworth, eds., *Through Dakota Eyes*, 26.

15. Ibid., 20, 24.

16. Ibid., 26.

17. Wabasha's Statement, in Anderson and Woolworth, eds., *Through Dakota Eyes*, 29.

18. Blegen, *Minnesota*, 267.

19. Folwell, *Minnesota* , 232.

20. Ibid., 236.

21. Big Eagle's Account, in Anderson and Woolworth, eds., *Through Dakota Eyes*, 56.

22. Introduction to Anderson and Woolworth, eds, *Through Dakota Eyes*, 5.

23. Gabriel Renville's Memoir, in Anderson and Woolworth, eds., *Through Dakota Eyes*, 189.

24. Samuel J. Brown's Recollections, in Anderson and Woolworth, eds., *Through Dakota Eyes*, 77.

25. Ibid.

26. Cecilia Campbell Stay's Account, in Anderson and Woolworth, eds., *Through Dakota Eyes*, 51.

27. Nancy McClure Faribault Huggan's Account, in Anderson and Woolworth, eds., *Through Dakota Eyes*, 244.

28. George Quinn's Account, in Anderson and Woolworth, eds., *Through Dakota Eyes*, 94.

29. Good Star Woman's Recollections, in Anderson and Woolworth, eds., *Through Dakota Eyes*, 53.

30. Samuel J. Brown's Recollections, in Anderson and Woolworth, eds., *Through Dakota Eyes*, 223.

31. Clara Janvier Kinkead, "Contemporary Account of Experiences in *The Sioux Uprising 1862*, by Clara Janvier Kinkead," in J. Eckman, *The Kinkeads of Delaware as Pioneers in Minnesota, 1856-1868* (Wilmington, DE: George W. Butz, 1949), 42.

32. Nancy McClure Faribault Huggan's Account, in Anderson and Woolworth, eds., *Through Dakota Eyes*, 244-245

33. Samuel J. Brown's Recollections, in Anderson and Woolworth, eds., *Through Dakota Eyes*, 74.

34. George Quinn's Account, in Anderson and Woolworth, eds., *Through Dakota Eyes*, 94.

35. Gabriel Renville's Memoir, in Anderson and Woolworth, eds., *Through Dakota Eyes*, 187.

36. Ibid.

37. Nancy McClure Faribault Huggan's Account, in Anderson and Woolworth, eds., *Through Dakota Eyes*, 244-245.

38. Folwell, *Minnesota*, 124.

39. *St. Paul Press*, August 30, 1862, in Meier, Newspapers, 58.

40. Kinkead, *Kinkeads*, 30-33.

41. Ibid., 34-35.

42. Anthony F. C. Wallace, *The Long Bitter Trail: Andrew Jackson and the Indians* (New York: Hill and Wang, 1993), 112.

43. *Mankato* [Minn.] *Weekly Record* , January 3, 1863, in Meier, *Newspapers*, 60.

44. *Faribault Central Republican*, August 27, 1862, in Meier, Newspapers, 60.

45. Oehler, *Sioux Uprising*, 207.

46. *Faribault Central Republican*, August 27, 1862, in Meier, *Newspapers*, 58.

47. In the week between September 28 and November 5, 1862, 392 Dakota men accused of committing aggressive acts against whites were tried by a five-man military commission. Three hundred and seven Dakotas were sentenced to death, and sixteen to imprisonment. All but thirty-nine of those sentenced to death had their sentences commuted by President Lincoln, though the remainder remained in military custody; one of the condemned thirty-nine men was granted a last-minute reprieve; Blegen, *Minnesota*, 279.

48. *Mankato* [Minn.] *Weekly Record*, January 3, 1863, in Meier, *Newspapers*, 60.

49. Little Crow to H. H. Sibley, September 7, 1862, in Heard, *History of the Sioux War*, 48.

Jerry L. Russell, Founder and National Chairman

THE STUDY OF THE MILITARY HISTORY of the early settlement of North America, and the continuing conflicts between Indian and Indian, Indian and settler, Indian and soldier, has long been a subject that has fascinated succeeding generations of Americans.

In the early decades of this century, an organization known as **The Order of Indian Wars of the United States**, made up primarily of retired military men, actual veterans of the Indian Wars, devoted its attention to the study of the U.S. military establishment's role in the development and settlement of this country's westward-moving frontier. That organization became an affiliate of the American Military Institute in 1947, and is once again active for descendants.

IN 1979, WE FOUNDED A **NEW** ORGANIZATION, inspired by that other group--a "spiritual descendant," if you will--but having no connection, official or otherwise with the predecessor. Our purpose, however, is similar--but broader: the in-depth study and dissemination of information on America's frontier conflicts. We are as interested in the "Indian side" as in the "Army/settlers side," although this organization, and its Assemblies, are not to be a forum for political or sociological crusades or guilt trips---our interest is in **military history**.

An additional purpose, equally important, we believe, is our concern for the historic preservation of those important sites associated with the history of the Indian Wars in America. Citizens' groups **must** become more involved in historic preservation, or much of our past will be irretrievably lost, in the name of 'progress'. Historic military sites are an important part of our national heritage, and the preservation/protection of these sites will be a major, continuing, concern of our organization--hence our motto: WE WHO STUDY MUST ALSO STRIVE TO SAVE! HERITAGEPAC is the national lobbying organization established in 1989 to work for preservation of battlesites. Our main publication is the *OIW Communique*.
DUES ARE $20 A YEAR.

Our 21st Annual National Assembly, Focusing on the 125th Anniversary of The Red River War, will be held September 16-18, 1999, in Amarillo, Texas, With Tours Led By Neil C. Mangum, Superintendent, Little Bighorn Battlefield, to Adobe Walls, Palo Duro Canyon & The Washita Battlefield, Plus 12 Speakers.
WRITE FOR INFORMATION.
Order of the Indian Wars
P. O. Box 7401, Little Rock AR 72217
501-225-3996   > indianwars@aristotle.net <

STAND WATIE
AND ELY PARKER

Patrick Bowmaster

To some, it seemed Gen. Robert E. Lee was startled when he noticed a dark-skinned man preparing the document of Lee's surrender. When the Southern general finally discerned the nationality of the Iroquois officer, Lee, with typical grace, said that he was "glad to see one real American here." The incident was one of the most notable in the life of Ely Samuel Parker. By the time of Lee's surrender, this Union colonel was, along with Confederate Brig. Gen. Stand Watie, one of the two highest-ranking members of an Indian nation to serve in the American Civil War. Their life stories represent an interesting historical contrast.

Stand Watie, who was three-quarters Cherokee, was born in the old Cherokee nation on December 12, 1806. His Indian name, Degataga or Takertawker, has been variously interpreted as "He Stands," "Standing Together as One," "Standing Together," "Stand Firm," or "Immovable." After graduating from a mission school, he went to work both on the family farm and his brother's newspaper, the *Cherokee Phoenix*. The paper was a vocal supporter of the "Treaty Party." This minority political faction, which was led by Watie's relatives and connections, favored selling the Cherokee homeland in present-day Georgia to the United States in return for a reservation in Indian Territory. They believed that the Cherokees would inevitably lose their land and that an immediate accord with the Federal government would leave their people with a much better arrangement than that which would be forced upon them if they waited until their land was taken against their will.

In 1835 Watie became one of the signers of the Treaty of New Echota. With this controversial document, Watie and the other members of his faction sold off all Cherokee land. This was done even though Cherokee law required death for any tribal member who gave up land without national authorization. The resulting Cherokee removal, via the infamous "Trail of Tears" to present-day Oklahoma, represented the subversion of the will of both the Cherokee government and some 90 percent of the nation's people. In 1839, their signing of the New Echota agreement cost three of Watie's relatives their lives and left the tribe gripped in a blood feud. Watie himself narrowly escaped assassins sent to kill him as a result of his role in the removal.

After this escape, however, Watie successfully spent the two decades prior to the Civil War as a clerk of the Cherokee Supreme Court, lawyer, plantation owner, merchant, and councilman and speaker in the Cherokee Nation Council. Through these endeavors he built a sizable fortune. He also held a leadership position in the Knights of the Golden Circle, an organization intent on fighting abolitionism among the Cherokees.

Like Watie, Seneca citizen Ely Samuel Parker belonged to a family that held a place in the political leadership of his nation. Born on the Tonawanda Reservation within New York State in 1828, Parker was given the Iroquois [Haudenosaunee] names Hasanoanda, "The Reader," or "Coming to the Front," or "Leading Name," and Donehogawa, "He Holds the Door Open," as well as an English language name.

Parker was educated at a mission school and two private academies. He would need this background, for in contrast to Watie's, Parker's legal and political activities took place in several different worlds. At only fourteen,

Brevet Brigadier General
Ely Samuel Parker

Brevet Brigadier Generals in Blue

Parker began serving in 1841 as a representative of his reservation's people and as interpreter to the governments of both Washington and the state of New York. Parker's linguistic skills were excellent and were a factor in his forming a relationship with Lewis Henry Morgan. Parker assisted Morgan, whom he met in 1844, as a researcher, interpreter, and ethnographic source during the preparation of Morgan's masterpiece *League of the Ho-de-no-sau-nee, or Iroquois*. Parker's contribution to the work was so great that he has long been recognized for his role in the founding of American anthropology.

Parker's brilliance was also a factor in his being selected as part of a delegation sent to Washington in 1846 to save the reservation land from avaricious whites. For years he returned to the capital, fighting for his peoples' lands and rights. In 1851, the Iroquois Confederacy or Six Nations made Parker a Grand Sachem, or high chief. This award, the highest given by the Six Nations, was tendered in appreciation for his indefatigable and expert service in their interests. The ongoing effort of Parker to save their reservation culminated in title to three-fifths of the remaining tribal land being secured in 1857. This success represented the highlight of Parker's efforts on behalf of the Six Nations.

During these activities, Parker also "read for the law," the practice through which most American attorneys received their legal education. However, Parker was not admitted to the New York bar because he was an Indian and therefore not considered a United States citizen. As a consequence, in 1849 he began supporting himself through a successful career as a self-taught civil engineer. It was while working as an engineer that Parker became a friend of a Galena, Illinois, clerk named Ulysses S. Grant in 1860. This association would be one of the most important developments in Parker's life.

The coming of the American Civil War in 1861 found Parker and Watie on opposite sides. Watie rallied to the Confederate standard. He initially served as captain of a company of Confederates whose aim was to guard the Indian Territory against Union forays. He later organized the First (later renamed Second) Cherokee Mounted Rifles Regiment and became its colonel on July 12, 1861. Watie participated in only one major battle, Pea Ridge, Arkansas, on March 7-8, 1862. There, his command captured and temporarily held a union battery and later adroitly covered the Confederate retreat from the field. [For a differing opinion on Watie's role, see the interview with Doug Keller in this issue.]

By May 6, 1864, Watie received promotion to brigadier general. The commission made him only the second individual with predominantly Indian ancestry to become a general in an American army. He was the only member of an Indian tribe to hold such high rank during the Civil War. As a general, Watie led the First Indian Brigade in the Trans-Mississippi Department of the Confederacy. His command included most, and by the end of the war, all, pro-Confederate forces from Indian Territory.

Watie was largely a guerrilla fighter and cavalry raider who performed exceptionally well in those roles. As a result, between 1862 and 1865 Watie forced the Union to divert thousands of soldiers from the front lines to his various areas of operation. His signal accomplishments were the June 15, 1864, seizure of the Union steamboat *J. R. Williams* and the capture of a Federal wagon train loaded with a million and a half dollars worth of supplies during the Second Battle of Cabin Creek on September 19, 1864. During the course of the war, his men participated in eighteen minor battles and significant skirmishes and many more small fights. On June 23, 1865, Watie became the last Confederate general to surrender, enhancing his fame as a result.

While hard fighting characterized Watie's conflict, paperwork was the mainstay of Parker's Civil War service. In 1862 Parker determined to land a commission in the Federal army. Prejudice toward his ethnicity and the fact that as an Indian he was not classified as a United States citizen thwarted his desire. Fortunately, his friend from Galena intervened on Parker's behalf. By then a brigadier general, Grant in 1863 helped Parker enter United States service as a captain with a commission dated May 25. As Grant's star rose, so did Parker's. Parker received assignment to the staff of Brig. Gen. J. E. Smith and served as an assistant adjutant general and engineer of the Seventh Division, XVII Corps, Army of the Tennessee.

In September 1863, Grant reassigned Parker to his personal staff. He became Grant's military secretary with the rank of lieutenant colonel on August 30, 1864. It was this promotion that eventually brought him into contact with Robert E. Lee. On April 9, 1865, Parker wrote out the surrender terms agreed to by Grant and Lee, the commander of the legendary Army of Northern Virginia. It was prior to the signing of the document that Lee told Parker he was "glad to see one real American here." Parker responded with equal grace by telling Lee, "We are all Americans."

Ely Parker subsequently received a brevet promotion to brigadier general of volunteers, back dated to the day of the surrender. Because a brevet promotion was little more than an acting or sometimes honorary rank, the reward did not give Parker the right to claim he had actually been commissioned a general. After the session of hostilities, however, Parker was promoted to the permanent rank of colonel of volunteers on July 25, 1866.

The triumph of Union arms began a period of rising fortunes for Parker and declining ones for Watie. When Cherokee Principal Chief John Ross and the majority of Cherokee people switched their allegiance from the Confederacy to the Union in 1862, Watie had become chief of the pro-Southern faction of western Cherokees. After the war he unsuccessfully attempted to persuade the Federal government to divide the Cherokee reservation in the Indian Territory between those who had supported the Confederacy and those who favored the Union.

With his diminishment in political importance, Watie was employed as a farmer and businessman in the post-Civil War years. During this period of his life he served as an ethnographic source, as Parker had done before him. His knowledge benefited the production of Henry Rowe Schoolcraft's *Information Respecting the History, Condition, and Prospects of the Indian Tribes of the United States*. This was one of the last notable events in Watie's life. He died in Indian Territory on September 9, 1871.

With the conclusion of war and the imminent dissolution of the volunteer army, Parker decided to remain in the military and continue as an aide to Grant. With Grant's help, Parker obtained a commission as a second lieutenant in the Second U.S. Cavalry Regiment of the regular army on March 22, 1866. He was later promoted to 1st lieutenant and on March 2, 1867, received brevet promotions through the ranks of captain, major, lieutenant colonel, and brigadier general for his years of distinguished service.

Upon Grant's election as president in 1868, Parker resigned his army commission to become the only Indian to ever hold the position of commissioner of the Office of Indian Affairs. His service in this capacity was exemplary as he strove to implement Grant's "Peace Policy" toward Western Indians. However, Parker's and Grant's political enemies forced a Congressional investigation into allegations of fraud against Grant in 1871. Although he was completely innocent of the charges and officially cleared of all wrongdoing, the attempt to destroy him left Parker so disgusted that he resigned the office. Parker next tried his hand in the business world, with mixed results. In 1876 he received appointment as a clerk for the Committee on Repairs and

Supplies of the New York City Police Board of Commissioners. He held this position until his death in Fairfield, Connecticut, on August 30, 1895.

Parker's and Watie's family affairs were as different as other aspects of their lives. Watie's family life is an interesting story in its own right. Prior to his tribe's being removed to Indian Territory, Watie married Eleanor Looney, Elizabeth Fields, and Isabel Hicks. It is known that his marriage to Fields ended with her death, but there is little other information available about the three relationships. He is believed to have had several children from the marriages, but they died young. In September 1843, Watie married for the last time, wedding Sarah Caroline "Betsy" Bell. Three sons (Cumiskey, Saladin, and Solon) and two daughters (Ninnie Josephine and Charlotte Jacqueline) were born to the couple. All three boys died in the 1860s, and his daughters survived Watie by only two years. His wife Sarah, however, outlived Watie by twelve years.

Parker's family life was more mundane. On December 25, 1867, he married a non-Indian Washington socialite named Minnie Orton Sackett. The couple had one child, a daughter named Maud Theresa, who was born in 1878. His wife would live until 1932 and his daughter until 1956.

For all of their differences, Stand Watie and Ely Parker are primarily remembered for the same reason. It is ironic that, given their unconquered spirits, both men are today best known for their attendance at a surrender.

Flowing With Blood and Whiskey

STAND WATIE AND THE BATTLES
OF FIRST AND SECOND CABIN CREEK

Palmer Boeger

After Cherokee-born Brig. Gen. Stand Watie's Confederate troopers seized 200 wagons from a Union supply train at Cabin Creek, Indian Territory, in September 1864, his men found barrels of whiskey while prowling through the captured cargo. To prevent mishaps while the train was moving to safety in Confederate territory, Watie ordered the barrels poured into the Verdigris River. Depriving his opponents of $1.5 million dollars in supplies and avenging an earlier defeat at Cabin Creek must have seemed intoxicating enough without the alcohol.

Although Cabin Creek was an unimpressive stream in 1862, the road crossing it was an important artery of travel. Known variously as the Military Road, Texas Road, Immigrant Road, or Osage Trail, it was already a much used wagon road south before the war arrived. When the first Union troops arrived in 1862, they found a thriving community already at the Cabin Creek crossing. The area was partially cleared for several farms, and livestock grazed in the open fields. In 1864, the road carried freight from Fort Scott to Forts Gibson and Smith. Running south, the Military Road forked at the Kansas line. The west branch ran along the west bank of the Grand River, the other branch to Fort Gibson.[1]

In the spring of 1862, the Federal command in Kansas dispatched forces to gain control of the Indian Territory south as far as the Arkansas River. Federal military and refugee camps in Kansas were frequently in a state of panic from rumors of imminent Confederate invasion. The first Union advance reached to

The crossing at Cabin Creek.
Courtesy of Michael A. Hughes

Tahlequah and Muskogee, but withdrew without accomplishing anything when the officers quarreled. A second attempt in the autumn of 1862 by Col. W. A. Phillips overran the hamlet at Cabin Creek and occupied the Cherokee capital of Tahlequah. In April 1863, Phillips went on to seize the military installation at Fort Gibson. The installation became headquarters for Union forces in the Indian Territory. On June 11, Gen. James G. Blunt, commander of the newly formed District of the Frontier, arrived at the fort determined to take the offensive.

The Federals at Fort Gibson had to solve a serious supply problem just to hold their position. A long column of Indian refugees, possibly as many as 15,000, had closely followed the Union army as it advanced south into Indian Territory. After two difficult winters in Kansas, the Indians hoped to go move south and reclaim their homes. To gather cattle and other subsistence from the reoccupied territory was out of the question. Two Federal invasions, foraging parties of the Union and Confederate forces, and marauding bands had cleared the area of almost everything edible. Most of the former residents had fled, leaving their cabins and taking what possessions they could carry. Now there was nothing left to return to. Attacks by Confederate bands, marauding parties, and bushwhackers kept the pro-Union refugees close to the army garrisons. To meet the crisis, an urgent call for supplies was forwarded to Fort Scott, Kansas. In response, the Federal command at the Kansas post began assembling a train of 200 wagons to be dispatched to Fort Gibson.

That same month, June of 1863, reports reached Kansas warning that the Confederates planned an attack to recover Fort Gibson. In response, a detachment of cavalry and a battery of artillery were ordered to reinforce the fort. The reinforcements would travel with the supply train. Anything that moved anywhere on the Military Road was subject to attack. However, intelligence reached the Federals that Stand Watie, the field commander of most Confederate troops in the Indian Territory, planned to intercept the train as it approached Fort Gibson. The train was therefore pushed hard, moving along with all possible speed, even traveling at night. If the wagons could be pushed at a rate of fifteen to twenty miles per day, they would complete their journey in five days. Mud and high water from recent rains slowed their progress, but the teamsters managed to locate high ground to detour around the worse spots as they creaked and rolled toward Fort Gibson. Troops from the wagon guard prowled patches of timber and growth along the road looking for signs of Watie and his men.

The Federals had good reason to fear Watie. The legendary cavalry raider and Georgia native was one of the signers of the 1835 treaty in which Cherokees agreed to give up their lands and move to Oklahoma—an agreement that triggered the infamous Trail of Tears. In his new home, Watie became a successful planter and led the minority faction when the Cherokee nation divided politically. Although the Cherokee were essentially neutral when the Civil War began, Watie convinced his followers to join the Confederate cause after the South defeated Gen. Nathaniel Lyon at Wilson's Creek in 1861. Watie raised the Cherokee Mounted Rifles and was appointed its colonel. An inspiring leader, he was best known for his hit-and-run tactics.[2]

The Confederate command at Fort Smith appreciated that if Fort Gibson remained in enemy hands, it would be utilized as a base of operations for launching a raid against the important Confederate base at Fort Smith, located on the Arkansas border. To counter this, Gen. William Steele, Southern

Brigadier General
Stand Watie

Generals in Gray

headquarters commander of the Indian Territory, determined to trap the supply train. Steele ordered Watie and Brig. Gen. William Cabell, the commander of Confederate troops in northwest Arkansas, to set up an ambush at the Cabin Creek crossing of the Military Road.

The Confederate generals promptly drew up a plan to snatch the wagons. Watie would assemble 500 of his troops, and Cabell would bring 1,500 men from Arkansas. The scheme required close coordination and good timing. Only Watie, however, was in position in time. Recent heavy rains and high water made it impossible for Cabell to cross Grand River in time to join the ambush. This left Watie with only a quarter of the men he and Cabell deemed necessary for the attack. Undaunted, Watie determined he would strike at the Cabin Creek crossing without Cabell's Arkansas soldiers.

On July 1, 1863, the Federal wagon train rumbled toward the crossing. Watie had deployed his main force in the timber on both sides of the Military Road, south (or below) the Cabin Creek ford. Confederate pickets were scattered on the north bank, well positioned to give advance warning of the train's arrival. As the train rolled within range, Watie's pickets went to work on the wagons and their teams. The surprised wagon guard, about 2,000 men composed largely of cavalry and the Second Kansas Battery, was led by Col. James A. Williams, commander of the First Kansas Colored Infantry. The escort included elements of the Ninth and Fourteenth Kansas Cavalry, the Third Wisconsin Cavalry, the Second and Third Indian Home Guards under Maj. John A. Foreman, and a few companies of the Second Colorado Infantry [Cavalry]. "[W]e came upon the enemy, strongly posted upon Cabin Creek, completely commanding the ford," Williams later reported. Much to Williams' dismay,

Watie's commanding position and Southern gunfire made it impossible for the train to cross the creek.[3]

Williams ordered his command to immediately deploy on the right and left of the ford. "We opened a brisk fire upon the enemy in the thicket on the opposite bank," recalled Major Foreman, "which we continued for half an hour." According to Williams, Foreman's effort killed three of Watie's skirmishers and captured three more, forcing the survivors to retire across Cabin Creek. "I ordered up one of the 12-pounder howitzers attached to my command, which, with the mountain howitzers of Maj. Foreman, opened a brisk fire of shell and canister, under the fire of which the soundings of the creek were taken," explained Williams. Unfortunately, the Federals discovered that the creek was "too deep to cross the train," and Williams ordered his men into camp "to await the falling of the stream, usually quite small, but now much swollen by the recent rains."[4]

That evening, Williams called a council of war with Lt. Col. Theodore H. Dodd, commanding the escort to the train, and Major Foreman. "It was determined to unite the different forces, as many as could be spared from the immediate defense of the train which had been corralled upon the prairie, about 2 miles from the ford," Williams later explained in his report. After conducting "a careful reconnaissance" that evening with both Dodd and Foreman at his side, Williams finalized his plan of attack. With the assistance of his artillery, Williams planned to force his way across the flooded stream. Two 6-pounders were dispatched to the extreme left of the line, while one 12-pounder howitzer and one mountain howitzer were unlimbered in the center, "directly in front of and not more than 200 yards from the position held by the enemy." The last piece, a 12-pounder howitzer, was deployed on the Federal right. Williams' plan was a bold one: his men would "attempt to cross the stream under the fire of these pieces."

Federal dispositions were completed about 8:00 a.m. the following morning. Shortly thereafter, Williams ordered his artillery to fire. "I opened a brisk cannonade, with shell and canister, upon the enemy's position, which was continued for forty minutes without interruption." According to Major Foreman, "The firing was continued about twenty minutes, when I received notice from the lookouts that the enemy were in disorder (not being able to see their movements from the creek, I had stationed a lookout or picket in some trees near Armstrong's battery)" on the right of the line. Foreman promptly informed Williams "that the enemy having apparently retired from his

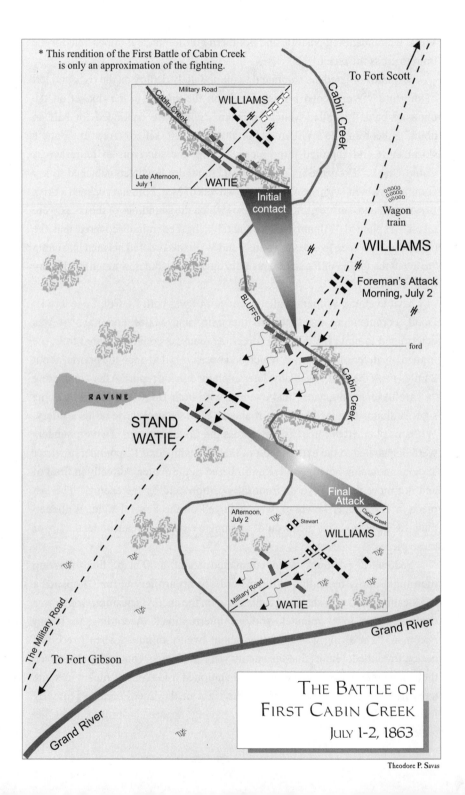

* This rendition of the First Battle of Cabin Creek is only an approximation of the fighting.

To Fort Scott

Cabin Creek

Military Road

WILLIAMS

Cabin Creek

Late Afternoon, July 1

WATIE

Initial contact

Wagon train

WILLIAMS

Foreman's Attack Morning, July 2

ford

BLUFFS

Cabin Creek

RAVINE

STAND WATIE

Final Attack

Afternoon, July 2

Stewart

WILLIAMS

Cabin Creek

Military Road

WATIE

The Military Road

To Fort Gibson

Grand River

Grand River

THE BATTLE OF
FIRST CABIN CREEK
JULY 1-2, 1863

Theodore P. Savas

position." Without hesitation, Williams "ordered the column forward, it having previously been ascertained that the creek had fallen sufficiently to allow a passage."[5]

Williams' column, led by Major Foreman, charged forward toward the ford. The men "had nearly reached the opposite shore," reported Williams, when "they were met by a violent fire of musketry from the enemy, who had concealed themselves behind logs in the thick brush which lined the opposite shore." Watie's Cherokees had not fallen back as previously believed. Caught in a vicious crossfire, Major Foreman "was twice shot by musket-balls, his horse receiving five shots." Foreman's wounding temporarily disrupted the advance. "Seeing their gallant leader fall, this advance company retired somewhat confusedly to the position formerly occupied by them," explained Williams. As Foreman remembered it, when "nearly across the creek, I was wounded, and obliged to go to the rear." Williams ordered a halt and filed the three leading companies to the right, where they "opened upon the enemy a fire of musketry." Federal artillery reopened as well, pounding Watie's men for twenty minutes. Shuffling his commands about, Williams ordered a new advance, "still keeping up the fire from the three companies of infantry, formed as before stated, and the howitzers. The enemy again opened fire, but did not succeed in checking our advance, and with the loss of but 3 or 4 wounded, I succeeded in crossing my column, the infantry wading to the arm-pits in water, and, driving the enemy from the brush, formed a line of battle directly in front of the enemy, who now formed in battle array about 400 yards in advance upon the edge of the prairie."

The climax of the engagement had now been reached. Watie, although outnumbered and heavily outgunned, refused to give up his commanding tactical position blocking the ford. Williams, knowing that he had to force a crossing and get the wagons to Fort Gibson, had to keep the initiative and drive Watie away. "I ordered two companies of cavalry, under Capt. Stewart, to take position on my right, to prevent any flank movement that might be attempted by the enemy in that direction," reported Williams after the fight. He also "ordered the company commanded by Lieutenant Philbrick to charge the advance line of the enemy, penetrate it, and, if possible, ascertain his strength and position, which was gallantly executed by the lieutenant." Philbrick charged head-on into the center of Watie's thin line. The Federal horsemen "broke it, and put him to flight. Seeing this, I ordered forward all the cavalry in pursuit of the now fleeing enemy," related Williams, "who were pursued for 5 miles, killing many and dispersing them in all directions."

Federal losses were only one killed and about twenty wounded. Watie's losses, however, are more difficult to determine. "The loss of the enemy is not definitely known," Williams reported, "but, from the best I am able to obtain, I think it will not fall short of 50 killed, as many more wounded, and 9 prisoners." Williams' estimation of Watie's strength was way off the mark—"from 1,600 to 1,800 consisting of Cols. Stand Watie's and McIntosh's Cherokee [and Creek] regiments, with detachment of 600 men from the Twenty-seventh [Fifth Texas Partisan Rangers] and Twenty-ninth Texas [Cavalry] Regiments." Since the "prime object was to conduct the supply train to your command," Williams wrote to his immediate superior, Col. William A. Phillips, "it was not deemed proper to cause any delay in pursuing the enemy."[6]

The arrival of the wagon train at Fort Gibson increased the garrison's confidence that the post could be held. Indian refugees huddling close to the fort—still variously estimated at 10,000 to 16,000—shared in the contents of the wagons. Looking to take the offensive, Gen. James Blunt planned to cross the Arkansas River and attack Confederate Gen. Douglas H. Cooper, commander of the First Brigade Indian Troops along Elk Creek twenty-five miles to the south. Cooper hastily assembled a large force of troops from Arkansas, Texas, and the Indian Territory to stop Blunt's projected Union offensive. On the night of July 15, Blunt crossed the river with a force of 3,000 men, primarily composed of black troops and Indians. Two days later, skirmishing broke out as Blunt's men approached Cooper's army of Choctaws and Cherokees. Although Cooper's men outnumbered the Federals, inferior weapons and damp powder doomed their efforts to defeat Blunt. After several hours of fighting, Cooper's Indians fell back, fighting a rearguard action as they retreated to safety. Honey Springs, the largest battle fought in Indian Territory during the Civil War (about 8,000 men combined), claimed 13 Federals killed and wounded and 47 captured; Cooper's losses are unknown.[7]

The Battle of Honey Springs gave the Union forces control of the Military Road back to the Kansas line, but Federal occupation of the Indian Territory north of the Arkansas River remained tenuous at best. The Confederates still had a strong presence in the open country. However, Union forces managed to establish regular traffic between Kansas and Fort Gibson. Couriers often traveled the route twice in a week. Wagon trains, usually of 200 wagons plus their cavalry escorts, rolled south from Fort Scott on a more or less regular basis. Columns of empty wagons were commonly seen returning on the road to Kansas.

After the engagement at Honey Springs, detachments of Union troops, usually a company or two in strength, were placed at "stations" along the road.[8] A detachment of 170 men was located at Cabin Creek station in November of 1863. This garrison constructed a stockade of heavy timbers set solidly into the ground. The ford had been a natural stopping place for emigrants and wagons before the war. This and the fact that it was the half-way point between Fort Scott and Fort Gibson made the Cabin Creek crossing a logical place to fortify. The precise size and location of that stockade are not remembered, but the timbers were described as twelve feet high, and the stockade as spacious enough to provide quarters for a hundred men and a hospital. A band of timber for construction ran eastward along the creek. To the south the country was open, with stretches of waist-high native prairie grass.

Union forces were hard pressed in the summer of 1864 to protect their wagon trains and hay stations. All supplies had to be hauled in, for the war had destroyed the territory north of the Arkansas River.[9] Two Federal invasions, foraging by Confederates, and thefts by swarms of bushwhackers left little on which to survive. Once plentiful, horses and cattle were gone. The area around Cabin Creek was typical of the region—it had been stripped bare. Most or all of the buildings of the village were gone. Despite this, in June the Federals sent down from Kansas to Indian Territory another 5,000 refugees that would have to be fed.[9]

The Federals could have brought supplies up the Arkansas River from Little Rock, but low water through most of the summer made it only barely possible for loaded steamboats to move upriver. Built out of planks and with steam pipe valves not well covered, river steamboats were vulnerable. In June, Stand Watie ambushed a steamer on the Arkansas, the *J. R. Williams*. Loss of the steamer further discouraged river traffic. Union forces would have to rely on wagons for supplies to Indian Territory.[10]

Confederate forces were also in bad condition. The Southerners were often dressed in rags, almost shoeless, wearing parts of uniforms, and armed with a variety of old weapons. Still, they kept the Unionists from wandering very far from their fortified posts. Raiding Confederate Regulars and bands of armed Confederate sympathizers threatened Federal communications, shot up hay camps, and tied down thousands of Federal troops. In July 1864, General Cooper operated around Fort Smith, driving in the pickets and causing some alarm. In August, Stand Watie with 500 men pulled off a raid at Gunter's Prairie, north of Arkansas. Watie seized prisoners, horses, and mules, burned hay, and caused further panic amongst his enemies.[11]

That same August, intelligence reached the Confederate camps that another large wagon train was being loaded at Fort Scott to be moved south down the Military Road to Fort Gibson. A few days after hearing of the train, Stand Watie—who had been promoted to brigadier general in May 1864—presented Brig. Gen. Samuel B. Maxey, his superior in the District of the Indian Territory since December, with a proposal for a major raid on Union communications and supply in the district. Watie had previously suggested an advance all the way into central Kansas, accompanied by raids on Union installations in Arkansas. General Kirby Smith, commander of Confederate forces west of the Mississippi River, approved of Watie going on the offensive. However, Smith had insisted that Watie's operations coincide with a planned last-chance invasion of Missouri by Maj. Gen. Sterling Price. In other words, any action by Watie would have to be undertaken by October 1. As a result, Watie scaled back his plans and proposed instead a raid on Union communications along the Neosho River and north of the Arkansas River. Such a raid would naturally include an attack on the supply train bound for Fort Gibson.[12]

Brigadier General Richard M. Gano, commander of a Confederate brigade assigned to Indian Territory, agreed to join with Watie on the projected looting

of the wagon train. Gano, a native of Kentucky and medical doctor before the war, joined John Hunt Morgan's cavalry shortly after hostilities began and participated in several raids. By 1863, Gano was the colonel of the Seventh Kentucky Cavalry. Shortly thereafter, he was reassigned to lead a mixed brigade of cavalry and artillery

Brigadier General
Richard Gano

Generals in Gray

in Indian Territory. His service during the Camden Expedition prompted Kirby Smith to promote him to general, a promotion which President Jefferson Davis confirmed in March 1865. The troops from Gano's and Watie's commands already shared a camp on the Canadian River, in the Choctaw Nation. On September 13, the two officers met at Camp Pike to formulate plans for their expedition. Watie had already agreed that since Gano outranked him—Gano was appointed general one month earlier than Watie—the Kentucky native should officially command the raid. However, the two men agreed at the start of the conference that each would keep field command of his own troops, though they would act together. This was a wise decision, for Trans-Mississippi and Indian troops often would not fight for anyone but their own commander.[13]

Stand Watie's Confederate Indian Brigade numbered about 800 men and consisted primarily of the First and Second Cherokee Regiments, the First and Second Creek Regiments, and John Jumper's Seminole Battalion. Richard Gano's 1,200-man Texas brigade consisted of the Twenty-Ninth, Thirtieth, and Thirty-First Texas cavalry regiments, a regiment made up of "Gano's Guards" plus part of Gano's old Seventh Kentucky Regiment, and Capt. Sylvanus Howell's battery of six guns. The combined brigades numbered about 2,000 men.[14]

Gano and Watie started north from Camp Pike on September 13, 1864, and soon reached the Creek Nation. Since the Confederate column was in constant danger of being detected as it moved north, Gano sent Maj. John Vann ahead with a Cherokee regiment to scout the area below the Arkansas River and also to look as far to the right (north) as possible. On the 15th, the Gano-Watie column crossed the Arkansas River near the Creek [Indian] Agency. Since the water in the Arkansas was high, the crossing took six hours to complete. The men on foot carried over the small arms ammunition in boxes held over their heads. Artillery rounds were transported on the backs of the horses. Scouts probed four miles from the column, but did not discover any Federals south of the Arkansas River. This meant that the column would be secure as it turned northward. That evening Gano and Watie camped their men at Camp Pleasant, four miles south of Chosky in the Creek Nation. At that point the Confederate raiders were just eleven miles northwest of Fort Gibson. It had taken two days to cover thirty-five miles.[15]

The Union wagon train hunted by Gano and Watie was on the alert for just such a move. The Federals knew that the Confederates were generally well informed of both the departures and arrivals of wagon trains from Fort Scott and

Fort Gibson, and the number of troops in their escorts. Major Henry Hopkins, who commanded the wagon train Gano and Watie were seeking, asked Federal station commanders along the route to scout their areas for Southern troops. All Union forces along the Military Road were put on high alert. As body of men as large as Watie's and Gano's could not go undetected for very long. On the morning of September 16, the Confederate column bypassed Fort Gibson, rode north and crossed the Verdigris River at the Sand Town Ford. Union scouts detected the crossing.

That afternoon, Confederate scouts searching for Hopkins' wagon train discovered a Union hay camp at Flat Rock Creek, just off the road some twelve or fifteen miles north of Fort Gibson and thirty-five miles south of Cabin Creek Station. Gano and Watie observed the Federal hay camp from a hill. Since such work camps were vulnerable, Federal commanders usually kept a ring of mounted scouts a few miles beyond the camps, watching the fords leading to them. Captain Edgar A. Barker, commanding at Flat Rock, had 125 men of the Second Kansas Cavalry and a detachment of the First Kansas Colored Infantry. When he was warned of the approaching Confederates by his scouts, Barker made a personal reconnaissance. To his dismay, the Confederates were just two miles away. "I immediately formed my men on a ravine in the rear of my camp, in the most advantageous position, to repel and attack or protect the hay, and, taking a squad of mounted men with me (the rest of the cavalry being dismounted), proceeded to reconnoiter for the enemy, and find out their number and designs. I met them about two miles from my camp, 1,000 or 1,500 strong, with six pieces of artillery."[16]

Realizing the perilous position his men were in, Barker "immediately fell back, skirmishing with their advance which made several unsuccessful attempts to cut me off from my camp, after reaching which I dismounted my men and placed them in the ravine with the others." Just after Barker's men settled into the ravine, "the main body of the enemy appeared and attacked me from five different points, their infantry line moving up to within 200 yards, while their cavalry made three distinct charges, but were each time handsomely repulsed by the colored infantry and dismounted cavalry," Barker later reported. His position, though, was hopeless:

> After fighting them for half an hour, and finding myself completely overwhelmed and surrounded, and my position every moment becoming more and more untenable, I determined to charge them with my mounted men, and order the infantry and dismounted cavalry to make the rest of their

way to the Grand River timber, about a mile distant. Mounting my men and selecting the weakest point in their lines, I made at them with a rush they could not withstand, and succeeded in cutting my way through, with a loss of all but fifteen men. The whole force of the enemy then charged into my camp, capturing all of the white soldiers remaining there, and killing all the colored soldiers they could find. Only four out of thirty-seven of them succeeded in making their escape. The enemy captured and destroyed all of my camp and garrison equipage, company books, and papers of every description pertaining to my company. Also a quantity of ordnance and ordnance stores . . . for which I was responsible. Also 12 U. S. mules and 2 6-mule wagons and harness, which were burned, together with all the mowing machines, wagons, &c., belonging to the hay contractors. My whole loss is 40 killed; wounded, missing, and prisoners, 66.[17]

Prisoners taken at Flat Rock soon revealed that the prized objective, the Union wagon train from Fort Scott, was expected to pass into Indian Territory at any time. Gano and Watie already knew that 200 wagons had rolled south from Kansas a month earlier, with the Second Kansas Cavalry acting as an escort. That train had been immediately unloaded at Fort Gibson. The Confederate officers now learned that those empty wagons had started back to Kansas several days before the Confederates arrived at Flat Rock. This gave Gano and Watie a good idea of the train's size and return date.

On September 17, the Southern column commenced the thirty-five mile ride to Cabin Creek Station. That night, Gano's force camped on Wolf Creek, near present-day Salina, Oklahoma. Now that they were in Union-held territory, there was a sense of urgency driving the Confederate troops. Gano and Watie extended their scouting of the Military Road to the Park Hill-Fort Gibson branch of the road east of Grand River, just in case the train had taken that route. There was some apprehension that the wagons had slipped through their grasp. That fear subsided when Confederate scouts reported that no wagons had passed east of Grand River. The ride to Cabin Creek was interrupted a dozen time with alarms in anticipation of the train's arrival. Whenever Federal pickets were spotted, Gano's and Watie's men naturally assumed that the elusive train was approaching. At one point, a detachment of Union soldiers was seen making hay on a farm known as the Hickey Place. Troops were sent to destroy the camp, but the attack was called off when someone realized it would take too long and discharging weapons might attract unwanted enemy attention.

Growing impatient, Gano on the morning of September 18 took an advance party of 400 men and moved up the Military Road in search of the train. While

Gano made his reconnaissance, Watie remained with the bulk of the troops. It was important that the main force not be detected. At three o'clock in the afternoon, Gano spotted the wagons parked at the Cabin Creek Station. The white canvas tops left no doubt in Gano's mind: the train been found. The wagons were spread out across the landscape—behind the stockade, in the timber along the creek and on its bluff, and for one and one-half miles northward along the road. Many were loosely parked in "open order" for a mile around the open prairie-like area south of the creek. Many had their mules unhitched, and horses were grazing unconcernedly in the open area. A thin Federal picket line was stretched around the wagons. Gano wisely hid his men in a depression in the prairie south of Cabin Creek and sent off an urgent dispatch to Watie to bring up the rest of the troops.[18]

The ill-fated supply train had departed Fort Scott on Monday, September 12. Major Henry Hopkins, commander of the Second Kansas Calvary Regiment and of the train and its escort, was a veteran of the battles at Honey Springs and Fort Wayne. He was responsible for 205 mule-drawn government wagons loaded with quartermaster and commissary supplies, as well as four ambulances and ninety sutlers' wagons. The quartermaster wagons carried clothing, blankets, and shoes, some of which were intended for the thousands of refugees huddling about Fort Gibson. Eighty men of the Second Kansas Cavalry, fifty from the Sixth Kansas Cavalry, and 150 of the Fourteenth Kansas Cavalry made up the wagon escort. Four hundred unarmed Federal recruits also came down with the train. Since Union headquarters for the District of the Frontier anticipated a Confederate attempt to intercept the wagons, every Federal post between Fort Scott and Fort Gibson had been placed on full alert before Hopkins' train had rolled a single mile.[19]

At Baxter Springs, Kansas, near the Indian Territory line, Hopkins picked up 100 pro-Union Cherokees to act as a rear guard for the train. Fifteen miles into the territory, at Hudson's Crossing on the Neosho River, a message from Fort Scott informed Hopkins that Confederate Maj. Gen. Sterling Price had moved north across the Arkansas River east of Fort Smith. This meant that if the train was attacked, it would not be by any troops from Arkansas, as they would be assisting Price's campaign. It also portended, however, an increase in Confederate activity in the Trans-Mississippi.

On September 18, Hopkins sent to Col. Stephen H. Wattles, commanding at Fort Gibson, a request that Wattles send all the men he could spare to reinforce the train. He expected to be attacked by a force greater than his own,

Hopkins explained. The reply was an ominous dispatch from Fort Gibson informing Hopkins that a Confederate force of 1,200 to 1,500 men was headed north in the direction of Cabin Creek. Hopkins was told that he must move the train to the stockade at Cabin Creek Station as rapidly as possible. Three hundred Cherokees from the Third Indian Home Guard Brigade would join him there. In addition, Maj. John Foreman (the same officer who had been wounded while serving so well at First Cabin Creek in 1863) would shortly be on his way with six companies of troops and two guns. Moving his wagons in a double column, Hopkins pressed ahead over the last fifteen miles. The first wagons arrived in mid-morning on September 18 and continued to come in throughout the afternoon hours. One hundred forty of the 300 reinforcements also arrived. These men, the 170 men of the Cabin Creek Station, plus the original wagon escort, gave Hopkins a total of 610 men to protect his valuable train.[20]

In the meantime, a Federal patrol spotted a group of Confederates concealed in a depression in the prairie grass about three miles to the south of the crossing. At 4:00 p.m., Hopkins, with a mounted patrol of twenty-five men of his Second Kansas Cavalry, undertook a personal reconnaissance. "Moving south from the station at Cabin Creek three miles, I found the enemy strongly posted in a hollow on the prairie," Hopkins later reported. Returning to Cabin Creek Station, Hopkins ordered a defensive deployment. The pickets were reinforced. A number of wagons were formed into a tight quarter circle behind the stockade. His troopers moved several of the hay ricks in front of the twelve-foot tall stockade, and others were moved to the right of the fortification. When the fighting began that night, the Confederates initially mistook the hay ricks for earthworks. Unbeknownst to the Federal commander, however, the few hundred Confederates manning the prairie depression constituted merely the advance of the Gano-Watie column and not the full extent of the enemy threat.

The stockade, the high bluff behind the stockade, two ravines, and the timber on and near the creeks all afforded cover for the Federal defenders. The stockade stood on a slight rise with its back to the creek. All of the buildings in it were fortified, including the 2-story house of Joseph L. Martin, known by some as "Greenbriar Joe." Hopkins was still unaware of the danger he faced when the clock passed midnight. His scouts guessed that they faced between 600 and 800 Confederates, and Hopkins did not expect an attack before daylight. His enemy harbored other plans.

In the bright moonlight, Watie brought up his warriors from their hiding places to the south across the open grassland. It was after midnight before the last of his troops were up. "After consultation we agreed to move on the enemy at once, who was aware of our approach, but entirely ignorant of our numbers," reported Watie. The decision to attack in the darkness rather than wait for daylight was unusual, and night attacks during the Civil War were very rare. Gano formed his command for battle and marched it quietly forward until it was about 500 yards from Cabin Creek Station. His Texas regiments formed the center and right of the Southern line. Watie's men of the Indian Brigade were placed on the left, facing the Federal right with the hay ricks and the wagons. His alignment included, from right to left, the First and Second Cherokee Regiments, Seminoles, Second and First Creek Regiments. Howell's battery took position in the center of the line. Two others were deployed to bombard the Union right. According to Union reports, the Southern battle line was two ranks deep, with mounted men in front and dismounted soldiers "a few paces in rear of the first."

The Confederate line was somewhat curved, and its flanks extended well beyond the Union defensive line. Still, Watie was not fully comfortable with the alignment. According to the Cherokee general, "The enemy had decidedly the advantage in position. Our men were formed on an elevated prairie that descended to the enemy's position on the creek. The moon, which shone very brightly, was in our rear. They thus had the double advantage of firing up hill with the moon and sky light."

Many of the Federals were well posted in the edge of the timber at the creek, taking advantage of the shelter provided by the bluff. Others crowded into the stockade for cover. "They also had the residence of Joseph L. Martin on the road strongly fortified with heavy timbers set upright in the ground," remembered Watie, a circumstance "that rendered them complete protection against small-arms."[21]

To Gano's surprise, an officer stepped out of the darkness and began a conversation with him. When the officer "learned that we were rebels," explained Gano, "he called on God to damn us, and invited us forward. I asked him if he would receive a flag from us. He said he would answer in five minutes. I waited fifteen, and hearing some wagons moving I advanced my line about 3 a.m." As they tramped across the prairie and down the slight rise in two long battle lines, the Confederates could see the silvery creek ahead in the bright moonlight. Gano's men struck first. When the Southerners approached "within

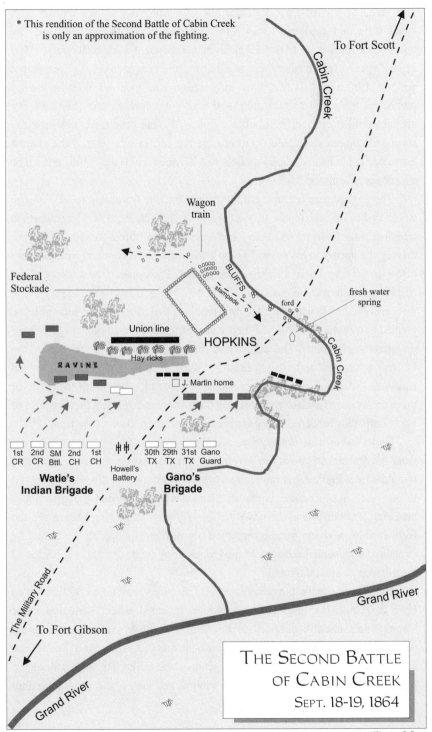

* This rendition of the Second Battle of Cabin Creek is only an approximation of the fighting.

To Fort Scott

Cabin Creek

Wagon train

Federal Stockade

BLUFFS

stampede

ford

fresh water spring

Union line

HOPKINS

Cabin Creek

Hay ricks

RAVINE

J. Martin home

1st   2nd   SM   2nd   1st   30th 29th 31st Gano
CR   CR   Bttl. CH   CH   TX   TX   TX   Guard

Howell's
Battery

Watie's   **Gano's**
Indian Brigade   **Brigade**

Grand River

The Military Road

To Fort Gibson

Grand River

THE SECOND BATTLE
OF CABIN CREEK
SEPT. 18-19, 1864

Theodore P. Savas

300 yards or less of their fortifications they opened fire. We replied with small-arms and artillery," was how Gano matter-of-factly described the opening of the battle. Major Hopkins remembered it a bit differently: "The enemy opened with artillery and small-arms, and moved upon my lines with a yell" at 1:00 a.m. "At that time information was received that the enemy numbered from 600 to 800 men, and was not informed that they had any artillery until it opened fire upon my lines." By that time there was little the surprised commander could do to change the course of events. "The nearest estimate I could form of their numbers was between 2,000 and 2,500 and four or six pieces of artillery."[22]

The engagement became general "along the line from right to left," Watie wrote in his official report two weeks after the action. "For a considerable length of time the firing was heavy and incessant. Our forces steadily advanced, driving the enemy to his cover." Gano's four artillery pieces had a devastating effect on what was now a tightly packed train. The noise of the artillery blasts and the exploding shells panicked the mules. The animals began to run; many were still hitched to wagons. Fleeing animals tipped over the wheeled-vehicles, tangled harnesses, and smashed their vehicles against trees. Some wagons were dragged over the bluff. The sudden and sharp rain of shells also frightened the Federal teamsters and wagon-masters who, explained a rather chagrined Hopkins, "with but very few exceptions, stampeded, taking with them one or more mules out of each wagon, leaving their trains and going in the direction of Fort Scott. This rendered it impossible to move any portion of the train."[23]

Under cover of darkness, reported Watie, Gano's men "drove the enemy from his [advanced] position, leaving in our possession a part of his train, around which a guard was immediately thrown and most of the wagons moved to our rear." At this time, however, Gano developed second thoughts about attacking a strong enemy he could not clearly see. "Not being able to see the fortifications, and having accomplished my design of stopping the train," he explained with some hindsight, "I moved my command back under the brow of the hill and awaited daybreak."

Gano's retrograde movement allowed Hopkins' embattled 400 troops to hold their position until daylight, which revealed what Gano and other Confederates initially believed to be "immense earth-works, but afterward proved to be immense hay ricks, ten in number, and just in the rear of said ricks a strong fortification constructed of logs set up in the earth." The timber along the bluff of Cabin Creek was "filled with wagons and mules, and from behind all these the enemy sent missiles of death." As the sun rose on September 20, the Confederates supposed, "from the noise in the enemy's camp, that he was crossing his train over the creek and moving it in the direction of Fort Scott." Gano ordered Watie to dispatch Lt. Col. John Vann "with the two Cherokee regiments across the creek on the left to gain the enemy's rear and intercept the trains. He gained the position," explained Watie, "but no wagons were crossing. He captured 18 prisoners." Watie also moved the Seminole Battalion to the left end of the Confederate line, along with some men of the Twenty-Ninth Texas. This extension of the line would enable him to sweep around the stockade and block avenues of retreat.

It was about this time, during a lull in the fighting just before dawn, that some of Watie's men got into a few wagons that they managed to seize beyond the Confederate left. Word got around that some of the sutlers' vehicles contained barrels of whiskey. Apparently some Union soldiers also found the refreshments, for some "well fortified" troops walked out into the night in the direction of the Confederate line. Several times, Watie's Confederate Cherokees crept up close to the stockade under the cover of darkness and made turkey gobbler calls. These calls were a challenge to a fight. The Union Cherokees sheltered inside the stockade replied in the same way.

According to Major Hopkins, at 7.30 a. m., the Confederates "advanced upon my lines, planting their artillery within 100 yards of my position." Both Watie and Gano confirmed Hopkins' observations: "After daylight we discovered the enemy's true position and moved a section of Howell's battery on the left, supported by the First and Second Creeks, and opened a vigorous fire from this advantageous position on his encampment and fortifications." The Confederates drove the Federal right 150 yards back, but were stalled by enemy soldiers sheltered in a ravine. We would have "carried the position but for a gully some twenty-five yards in the rear filled with armed men who had not yet participated," Gano wrote. "They were not visible until within twenty-five or thirty yards of them. We were compelled to fall back, but not one man of the gallant Thirtieth [Texas] started from that murderous fire until I ordered them to do so."

Realizing that victory was within his grasp, Gano ordered in his four Texas cavalry regiments and placed them on the extreme left of the Confederate positions. Gano led the attack personally. With assorted loud shouts, including "Rebel yells," the Texans charged. After replenishing their ammunition, the Seminoles joined in the final drive against Hopkins' position. The Federal defense began collapsing under the unrelenting pressure. Routed Federals ran through the wagons, through the stockade, and into the timber along the creek bottom. "Soon the confusion became great in his ranks and a general stampede ensued," remembered Watie, "leaving in our possession his train, stockade, hay, camp and garrison equipage." The Seminoles drove all of the way to the road, hundreds of feet away. Behind the fleeing Federals, Watie's Cherokees fired the hay ricks, which created additional confusion. By 9:00 a.m. the Federals had been driven from the field, leaving their wagon train—as well as dead and wounded—for anyone who might want it. "Our forces were compelled to fall back in disorder," Major Hopkins wrote simply, "leaving the train, with exception of a few wagons and an ambulance that moved back on the Fort Scott road."[24]

All semblance of organization among the Federals disintegrated in the confusion of the rout. The flying Union troops broke up into small parties. Most of the refugees tried to escape across the creek and flee north along the road to Fort Scott. Any hopes that Major Foreman's relief companies would arrive and that a part of the train might be recovered soon vanished. Many of the Federals hid in the timber and waited until the danger passed. Foreman would not arrive until the next day, in time to salvage a few wagons and some scattered supplies that the hurrying Confederates had not had time to load up. Union escapees from the disaster drifted into Fort Gibson and Baxter Springs for another week. Considering the fierceness and duration of the fight, casualties were light. Major Hopkins claimed his "killed, wounded, and missing [did] not . . .exceed 35 men," though Gano claimed he captured twenty-six Union prisoners in addition to the Federals killed and wounded. "The killed of the enemy at Cabin Creek numbered about 23," Gano wrote in his report. "The wounded not known; captured 26. The jaded condition of our already weak horses prevented us from capturing as many as we might have done. Our loss was 6 killed, 48 wounded—3 mortally."[25]

The victorious Confederates did not pursue the fleeing enemy very far. Everyone was aware that Federal troops were near and could appear at any moment. In addition, the Confederates quickly joined in looting the captured wagons. The captured vehicles were a real prize. "At 9 o'clock (six hours after the first volley was fired) the field was ours, with more than $1,000,000 worth of Federal property in our hands," reported General Gano with some pride. "We burned all the broken wagons and killed all the crippled mules. We brought off 130 wagons and 740 mules. We clothed 2,000 men of the expedition so as to make them comfortable for the present and have some commissaries on hand." Eventually, a figure of $1,500,000 later became the accepted value of the contents won that day.[26]

There was little time for an immediate inventory, however, as it was urgent to move the wagons out before a Federal relief column could arrive. Because of the need for haste, the Confederates made off with what could be most quickly salvaged. Their own artillery and the stampeding mules had made a shambles of the train. They righted overturned wagons, repaired broken wagon boxes, and replaced the broken wheels and poles on usable vehicles with wheels and poles from those that were not repairable.

Gano and Watie began to move out just two hours after the fighting ended. Badly broken wagons were burned and, Watie recorded, "a great many" mules were shot. Federal hay-making machines and hay ricks were burned, along with the papers and articles of the Cabin Creek post. With their captured wagons the Confederate column moved slowly southwesterly. The pace was determined by the ability of the jaded mules to pull the heavy wagons. Arriving in the area the next day, Major Foreman found supplies and a number of broken or abandoned wagons strewn for miles along the path of the captured train.

Even as the last wagons departed Cabin Creek, Confederate scouts sighted a Union relief force coming in from the east. These first pursuers were from the Seventy-Ninth Colored Infantry Regiment, an experienced unit commanded by Col. James M. Williams. It had been Williams and his troops who had defeated Stand Watie at the First Battle of Cabin Creek in July 1863. At 4:30 p.m. near Pryor's Creek, Williams' pursuit caught up with the Confederate train robbers. There were artillery exchanges for an hour. The running fight continued until nightfall. As darkness came on, the Confederate rear guard charged the approaching Federals, checking the pursuit, though Williams drove his attackers off with his Parrott guns. Camped on the George May farm that night, the Confederates ran a wagon back and forth over some rocky ground and built huge fires, all in an attempt to make their pursuers believe that they were parking their wagons for the night and preparing to fight in the morning. Instead, the Confederates resumed their flight in the predawn darkness.

Watie and Gano crossed Pryor Creek early on September 19 and headed west towards the Verdigris River. The column crossed the river at Clem Rogers' Place, near Claremore Mound, on the 21st. (Clem Rogers, another Cherokee Confederate office, would later be best known as the father of humorist Will Rogers.) It was here that Watie discovered that his Cherokees had recovered whiskey from the sutlers' wagons. Recognizing what the alcohol could do to discipline and morale on the march, Watie ordered the whiskey dumped into the Verdigris. Turning south, Gano's and Watie's men crossed the Arkansas River at Tulseytown (present-day Tulsa). After three days of headlong flight, the crossing ensured that the train was now safe from further pursuit. The Confederates, through heroic exertions in moving the wagons, had gotten away with about one-third of them.[27]

The Battle of Cabin Creek did not alter the course of the war. In the long run, the loss of the train was only a temporary setback for Union supply efforts in Indian Territory. However, reports of the raid caused a near-panic along the Kansas line and in southwestern Missouri all through October. Reports had Watie planning attacks on a dozen places. Federal troops were under constant alert, and soldiers needed elsewhere were shifted to the border of Indian Territory.

The victory was also a bright spot for Confederate sympathizers, especially since it came when the war back east was not going well and a month before Price's last-chance campaign in the West failed. For the pro-Southern people of the Indian Territory, half-starved and demoralized, their land devastated, the success provided a brief moment of elation. Watie and Gano received a flood of congratulatory orders, and the Confederate Congress gave Watie and his troops a vote of thanks.

A standard reference on the Civil War, *A Compendium of the War of the Rebellion* by Frederick H. Dyer, lists a total of forty-four military engagements in the Indian Territory (modern Oklahoma) during the war. Of these, Second Cabin Creek stands as the Confederacy's most significant victory in the Indian Territory and one of the greatest Confederate triumphs in the Trans-Mississippi West. It also ranks as the most impressive accomplishment by an American Indian officer during the American Civil War.

NOTES

1. Grant Foreman, *Down the Texas Road; Historic Places Along Highway 69 Through Oklahoma*, (Norman: University of Oklahoma Press, 1954).

2. Patricia Faust, ed., *Historical Times Illustrated Encyclopedia of the Civil War* (New York, 1986), 807-808.

3. United States War Department, *War of the Rebellion: A Compilation of the Official Records of the Union and Confederate Armies*, 128 vols. (Washington, D.C.: Government Printing Office, 1880-1901), vol. 22, part 1, 380. Hereinafter cited as *OR*.

4. Ibid., 380, 382.

5. Ibid.

6. Ibid.

7. Faust, *Encyclopedia of the Civil War*, 368.

8. Circular, General Orders No. 11, U.S. Army, Maj. Gen. [James G.] Blunt, Fort Scott, August 22, 1863; copy in the library of the Gilcrease Museum, Tulsa, Oklahoma.

9. Wiley Britton, *Memoirs of the Rebellion on the Border* (Chicago: Cushing, Thomas, 1882), 304; *OR* 34, pt. 2, 918.

10. Ibid., 41, pt . 3, 300.

11. Ibid., 997-999.

12. Ibid., 24, pt. 2, 945-946.

13. Ibid., 41, pt. 2, 1082; pt. 1, 780-782, 785. Gano's and Watie's camp was near present-day Stigler, Oklahoma. Brigadier General Samuel Maxey is the source for claiming Watie agreed to serve under Gano's command at Second Cabin Creek. According to Watie's report, however, the command situation was on an equal footing: "By an arrangement with Gen. Gano each one of us was to command his own troops, but act together and harmoniously. This we concluded to be the better plan, as the two brigades did not belong to the same division and were temporarily thrown together. I have had no cause to regret this arrangement, the conduct of Gen. Gano on all occasions being such as might be expected of so gallant an officer." Ibid., 785. Historian Anne Bailey, in *The Confederate General*, 6 vols. (Harrisburg, 1991), vol. 2, p. 150, claims Gano agreed to serve under Stand Watie.

14. Ibid., 41, pt. 1, 785. Gano's Brigade was primarily composed of Texans. The exception was a regiment which combined a two-company battalion of Texans known as "Gano's Guards" with eight companies of the Seventh Kentucky Cavalry Regiment. Gano had commanded the Seventh Kentucky in campaigns in Tennessee, and when he was transferred to the Trans-Mississippi theater of the war, he brought the Kentuckians with him. See Marcus J. Wright and Harold B. Simpson, eds., *Texas in the War, 1861-1865* (Hillsboro, Texas: Hill Junior College Press, 1965), 126.

15. Ibid., 41, pt. 1, 791.

16. Ibid., 771-772. The Flat Rock hay camp was located on the west side of Grand River, about five miles northeast of present-day Waggoner, Oklahoma.

17. Ibid. While relations between Confederate soldiers and black troops were seldom good, there were particularly deep animosities between the Confederate units at Flat Rock and the First Kansas Colored Infantry. The Twenty-Ninth Texas Cavalry had been badly shot up by the First Kansas at the Battle of Honey Springs, and the Texas cavalrymen had lost their flag in that action. Choctaw-Chickasaw units also seemed to bear the First Kansas a grudge; some members had previously been involved in a massacre of soldiers of the First Kansas during a wagon raid at Poison Springs, Arkansas, on April 18, 1864. According to one account: "Gano and Watie galloped their

line to within rifle range, then unlimbered their cannon. A few grape shots scattered the Federal guard, and the exultant victors rode unopposed into the hay-cutters camp. With guns across their saddles, the ragged Confederate Indians jogged up and down through the uncut hay and tall weed patches, shooting hidden Negroes like jackrabbits. Some black men rose from the weeds calling, 'O! Good master, save and spare me,' but all were shot down. Some were found submerged in the water under the creek banks, only their noses above the surface. These were killed like the others and their bodies dragged out onto the pebble bars." See Jay Monaghan, *Civil War on the Western Border* (Lincoln: University of Nebraska, 1955), 308.

18. Ibid., 766-771.

19. Ibid.

20. Ibid.

21. Ibid., 771-794.

22. Ibid., 767-768, 790. According to Watie's report, *OR* 41, pt. 1, 786, the advance began two hours later, or 3:00 a.m.

23. Ibid, 768, 786.

24. Ibid.

25. Ibid., 771, 791. See also, Britton, *The Union Indian Brigade in the Civil War*, 373. See also Jess C. Epple, *Battle of Cabin Creek, September 18,19, 1864* (Muskogee, Okla.: Hoffman Printing, 1964); Stella E. Carselowey Crouch, *Story of the Cherokee Indians, and "The Trail of Tears," "Battle of Cabin Creek"* [and] *"Allotting of Lands"* (Vinita, OK: n.p., 1964).

26. Ibid., 791, 792.

27. Ibid., 787-788, 791.

22. Frederick H. Dyer, *A Compendium of the War of the Rebellion,* 3 vols. (1909; reprint, Dayton, Ohio: Press of Morningside Bookshop, 1979), vol. 2, 985-987.

WESTERN AMERICAN INDIANS
DURING THE AMERICAN CIVIL WAR, 1861-1865

Michael A. Hughes

"Nothing lives long except the earth and the mountains."

I. Introduction

The Cheyenne leader White Antelope spoke truly as he calmly chanted his death song one winter's day in 1864: "Nothing lives long," including historical memory. For example, most Americans today can recall few events that took place west of the Mississippi River in the first half of the 1860s. With the exception of the Sand Creek Massacre, at which White Antelope was killed, this lapse in memory includes most of the Indian conflicts during that demi-decade in the West.

One reason for the obscurity of the Indian wars of the 1860s is that many of them took place within the overwhelming context of the American Civil War. During the war to determine the future of America, dozens of native nations were either swept up in the great contest or were participants in smaller but no less disastrous conflicts.

There were two different Indian populations at war. One populace lived west of the ninety-fifth meridian, the line of longitude running north-south down the center of North America. West of this line, groups of native peoples, many completely or semi-migratory, fought to preserve their ranges and resources and to carry on their traditional way of life. Some of these groups had already been engaged in hostilities with white miners and settlers as well as the army. Although their struggles took place apart from the Civil War, the conduct of these clashes was constantly complicated by the fighting taking place in the East. As a result, the 1861-65 Indian wars developed a breadth, savagery, and longevity they probably would not have had otherwise.

The other Indian population consisted of nations in states east of the Mississippi River and of eastern tribes relocated to reservations in Indian Territory [present-day Oklahoma]. This second population was largely sedentary and generally lived in, or largely surrounded by, white communities. Whether reservation Indians, tenacious remnants of dispossessed nations, or "assimilated" members of white society, this second population usually survived more by accommodation than resistance. As a result, some 20,000 Indian Territory and eastern Indians were drawn into the Civil War as soldiers or auxiliaries of the United States or the Confederacy.

Though obscured by the war in the East, the Indian conflicts of 1861-1865 in the West were among the most singular, devastating, and significant in American history. Unlike those of the 1870s, many of the Civil War-era Indian conflicts were new developments. During this period, a number of Western native nations were actively at war with the United States for the first or only time in their history. These "wars within a war" were in many cases unusually costly and unrestrained. The percentage of casualties in some Indian wars battles of 1861-65 greatly exceeded that of many large Civil War battles in the East. At Birch Coulee, Minnesota, for example, state volunteers suffered a 55 percent casualty rate in just the initial charge when attacked by Dakota warriors. Perhaps no other period in the warfare of the latter 1800s was so clearly genocidal. Of the five Indian wars incidents most frequently labeled "massacres," the two that are almost universally decried as slaughters were committed during the Civil War by volunteer regiments. At Bear River, Idaho, as least 250 of the 450 Shoshones present were cut down; at Sand Creek, Colorado, 150-200 of roughly 550 Cheyenne and Arapaho were killed and mutilated.

Despite these heavy losses, most Western engagements during the Civil War proved more inflammatory than conclusive. Many of the wars and battles were significant because of their lingering consequences. The mutual provocations committed during 1861-1865 led to cycles of costly reprisals that kept the West in turmoil for decades. This is especially true of the two longest and most costly series of Indian conflicts, those with the "Sioux" and the

Apache. Of all the wars within a war, only the one waged between the army and the Navajos reached a definitive conclusion.

West of the ninety-fifth meridian, competing armies of whites and disunited bands of Indians fought one another in bitter competition during the Civil War. Mescalero Apaches, for example, attacked Confederates in 1862 and then fought in 1864 the same Union troops that had opposed those Confederates. Indian troops in the [Oklahoma] Indian Territory and east of the Mississippi River fought with white compatriots against other enrolled Indian and white troops. Yet, these enlisted Indian soldiers were caught up in a war that was not their own. Their white counterparts professed that they were fighting a great crusade over the issues of secession, slavery, and states' rights. For the eastern and Indian Territory Indians, however, the war represented a last opportunity to avoid dispossession, division, and destitution.

Chaos and poverty were the invariable results of the United States policy innocuously termed "Indian removal." The hope of avoiding removal westward from their homes was the most important motivation for Indian service in the Civil War. It is almost impossible to overstate the amount of psychic, economic, and physical damage suffered during removals. The ethnic and religious identity of many Indians came from living at a geographical center point or point of origin described in legend. Such homelands were also the place of the graves of guiding ancestors. Even "assimilated" or "acculturated" Indians felt a sense of emotional displacement when leaving such locations. It is little wonder that the animosity between Indians who capitulated and signed removal treaties and those who refused split some nations for generations.

When Indians were forced to leave ancestral lands, they were often paid larcenously low prices for that land by state and federal officials. In addition, some or all of the annuities promised as compensation were usually diminished, diverted, or pocketed by agents and traders. The lands west of the Mississippi River to which the nations were moved were granted to them in part because the areas were considered so marginal in quality that whites would not desire to live upon them. But worst of all, removal was—however unintentionally—a murderous process. In the most notorious of these removals, those of the "Five Civilized Tribes" from the southern United States to the Indian Territory, each nation lost 12 to 20 percent of their members. In the one great removal during the Civil War, the Navajos' "Long Walk," the death rate was similar.

Indian peoples already in the West were also at risk. As soon as Nebraska and Kansas were organized into territories in 1854, their settlers' representatives began demanding the removal of all Indians to the Indian Territory. This would in turn require dislocating the nations within Indian Territory. As a result, both eastern Indians and Indian Territory Indians wished to win the favor of civilian and military authorities who might protect them against the forces of westward exile. The outbreak of the Civil War complicated the question about whose favor should be curried: the forces of the United States or those of the secessionist Confederacy?

The enormous complexity of the wartime situation for eastern and Indian Territory Indians is well illustrated by the case of the Cherokee. Many Cherokee men in present-day Oklahoma went from being neutral protectors of the Cherokee Nation, to allies of the state of Texas, to soldiers of a Confederate protectorate, to enemies of the state of Texas and the Confederacy. Meanwhile, many eastern Cherokee men in North Carolina and Tennessee fought alongside the soldiers of states that had formerly stolen their lands and denied them self-government. Remarkably, the eastern Cherokee did so in hopes that the "sovereign rights" the Southern states had claimed when attacking the Cherokee might also be asserted to protect Cherokee autonomy. In an ultimate irony, the Indian Territory Cherokee, most of whom fought *for* the United States, were punished after the war by federal land confiscations. Meanwhile, the eastern Cherokee, all of whom fought *against* the United States, were rewarded with the overdue honoring of federal treaty obligations.

Regardless of the outcome of the War Between the States, it was the Indians who were the surest losers. As Laurence M. Hauptman had noted in *Between Two Fires: American Indians in the Civil War*, the Civil War was the "final nail in the coffin in Indian efforts to stop the tide of American expansion." Eastern Indians, with the sole exception of the eastern Cherokees, discovered that loyal service to the United States or Confederacy did not provide them with additional political security or a release from poverty. Tribes of the Indian Territory, whether hostile or friendly to the United States during the conflict, were all punished after the war by expropriations of their land. Post-war Republican domination of Congress gave the Republican representatives of Kansas the power to press President Andrew Johnson into extinguishing most of the Indian reservations in that state. Nebraska followed suit in the 1870s. In the punitive Treaty of Washington of 1866, the United States required the sale of half of the land of the "Five Tribes" in the Indian Territory to make room for dispossessed Kansas and Nebraska Indians. Most of the Five Tribes' acreage was taken at non-negotiable and unreasonable prices. Large numbers of tribe members were forced to resettle for the second or even third time in their lives. The government also seized two right of ways for railroads through Indian Territory without compensation, opening routes for future white invasions of Indian land.

Other western Indians were less directly but no less certainly victims of the Civil War. The wartime shakeup in Congress enabled the passage of long-delayed legislation to approve and support the first of what would become five transcontinental railroads. The first route, across the central Plains, was completed by 1869. The "Pacific Railway" immediately began to further the destruction of the continental bison herd, the further division of the Cheyenne and Arapaho tribes, and the invasion of the Plains by ranchers. The war also left Western Indians facing a larger, more experienced, better armed, and more mobile Western army than they had faced before the war. Ominously, the Western Indian nations confronted a confident United States capable and willing of bringing about its territorial unification by any means possible.

Territory was not the only Indian possession that would come under attack. The election of President Abraham Lincoln in 1860 put in place a president who stated clearly that Indians must assume a white lifestyle. "I can see no way in which your race is to become as numerous and prosperous as the white race except by living as they do," Lincoln once advised Indian representatives. Lincoln's successors held the same view (as had the Confederates, as indicated in their Indian treaties). After the victorious commander of Union forces, Ulysses S. Grant, was elected president in 1868, the "assimilation" of the Indians became official United States policy. In the end, the Civil War did not simply cost the Indians lives and land. Its outcome threatened their very identity as Indians.

II. Western Indian Peoples and Their Wars in the Civil War Period

There were at least five major factors encouraging frequent and intense Indian conflicts with Indian peoples west of the ninety-fifth meridian during the Civil War: 1) the withdrawal of the U.S. Army from its garrisons in the Far West; 2) disunity in Western defense against the Indians; 3) the suspension of, or delay in, the United States government's meeting of treaty obligations to the tribes; 4) the increased role of state and civilian authority in the West; and 5) a coincidence of demands upon Indian lands and resources, generally as a result of mineral finds.

When fighting broke out between Union and Confederate forces in the East in the spring of 1861, all but a token force of U.S. Army Regulars or professionals were sent eastwards to fight or to organize and lead volunteers. (In addition, many officers, though not enlisted men, resigned their commissions in order to fight for the Confederacy.)

Most United States history books simply state that the troop withdrawal was the reason for the Western Indian wars of 1861-1865. The implication is that without the military to serve as a deterrent, Western Indian peoples fell back into earlier patterns of raiding and aggression. The troop removal was an important factor in the conflicts, but seldom as directly as is usually assumed. There are three common misconceptions about the impact of these transfers.

The first misconception is that the consequences of the troop transfers were rapid. In fact, except for the conclusion of some prewar operations in California, almost no fighting took place between the military and the Indians during the first year of the Civil War. Moreover, many Western Indian groups that had been fighting the United States actually broke off hostilities for at least one to three years. There were probably many reasons for this. Some peoples, such as the Navajos, Comanche, and Kiowa, may have welcomed the opportunity to recuperate from prewar military campaigns. Other nations, such as those of the Lakotas and Cheyenne, may have been content with the fact that the troop pullout was accompanied by a temporary reduction in civilian invasions of their territory.

The second misconception about the withdrawal of Regular troops was that the West was left ungarrisoned for a prolonged period. This is not true. At first, the withdrawal was covered by a limited redistribution of troops from the Department of California. Later, some of the absent Regular troops were replaced by "galvanized Yankees," Confederate prisoners of war willing to enlist in the United State Army to fight on the Western frontier. In addition, some U.S. Regulars remained in the West as members of state volunteer versus Federal regiments. By switching to state organizations, they could claim enlistment bounties, collect higher pay, and have a better chance of promotion. Most of the wartime manpower came from the recruitment of new state and territorial volunteer regiments. Around two dozen of these were utilized, two from as far away as New York and Massachusetts. The brunt of the fighting in the West was carried on by Union volunteer regiments from California,

Colorado, Minnesota, and New Mexico. With the state regiments taken into account, there were *more* soldiers fighting Indians during the Civil War than prior to the Civil War. In 1857, for example, there were only 11,000 soldiers in the entire region west of the Mississippi River; by 1862, that number had risen to 15,000 soldiers on the frontier, and 20,000 by the time the war ended in 1865.

In a number of instances, warfare in the West intensified—not because there were fewer troops, but because the replacement soldiers were state volunteers instead of U.S. Army professionals. The use of the volunteers was absolutely unavoidable. But several factors made them the worst possible troops to use in a critical period or in sensitive situations. Western volunteers were much more likely to be young, undisciplined, and violence-prone than were Eastern recruits. Some were young men who had left the restraints of family and community in the East, while others had grown up in the frequently mobile and insecure conditions of life in the West. Many Western volunteers were inured to seeing and committing violence well before their first Indian battle. Some men had been schooled in brutality while participating in prewar fighting in "Bleeding Kansas" or the nearly routine killing of Indians in the gold fields. The fact that members of the First New Mexico and Third Colorado cavalry regiments attempted to murder (or did murder) whites who criticized their treatment of Indians says something about the temperament of Western volunteers.

There were, of course, many decent and honorable men among the state volunteer regiments. It could also be argued that the violence and lack of restraint of the recruits came partially in response to their facing Indian opponents of whom the same was true. Still, some of the frequency and intensity of the Indian conflicts of 1861-1865 can be explained by the fact that state volunteers were more likely to provoke conflict and mistrust than were professional soldiers.

The third misconception about the withdrawal of the frontier Regulars is that the Western Indians always welcomed the professional troops' removal. In fact, some Western Indian groups were actually angered when the Regular troops were transferred. The frontier army had occasionally been used by Washington as an instrument of brute force in the interests of expansion. But the U.S. Army had also been in a peacekeeping role on behalf of some Western Indians. The army had protected Indian Territory tribes from raids by aggressive Plains tribes. It had also refereed or mitigated conflicts between traditional enemies. In addition, part of the military's mission was to restrict white civilian traffic and settlement to areas stipulated in treaties. When the professional soldiers were withdrawn, some Indian nations regarded the abandonment as a betrayal. Matters became worse when the professionals were replaced by state and territorial citizens already hated by the Indians.

A second major factor in 1861-1865 Indian conflicts, often overlooked, is the enormous wartime disunity in Western defense against the Indians. The best example of the problems this could create occurred in the south central United States. In the spring of 1861, the Indians of this region became the first to see U.S. Regular Army posts abandoned, the result of a premature surrender of federal facilities in Texas. Later that year, a Confederate expedition into New Mexico Territory resulted in fighting between Federals and Confederates on the Rio Grande. In March of 1862, the Confederate drive up the river towards Santa Fe was finally stopped. The arrival of the "California Column" of Union volunteers in New Mexico in May caused the Confederates to withdraw all the way to San Antonio, Texas.

By the summer of 1862, many Apaches, Comanche, and Kiowa had seen graphic evidence of just how divided their opponents were. They had seen white men drive one another from key frontier defense posts and then slaughter each other whenever and wherever possible. The Indians watched as rival armies left an area 500 miles wide largely defenseless, all the way from the Rio Grande in New Mexico east to the towns of Fort Worth and San Antonio in Texas. As a consequence, the Apaches and Comanche were handed a magnificent opportunity to resume the time-honored tradition of raiding without fear of retribution. At this point, the national disunity that had made new Indian conflicts possible made them almost unstoppable. Instead of the war zone being at the center of a single country, it was now as far as possible from the men and supplies of two rival countries. The Confederates could not readily get men and supplies to west Texas, because it was at the extreme western end of their supply lines. To make matters worse, growing Federal control of the Mississippi River and Confederate commitment to battles in the East meant that the state of Texas received but little outside help. Things were not much easier for the Federals. Any troops sent from the East had to bypass Confederate-held Texas and the [Oklahoma] Indian Territory. Most of the men and supplies who would fight in the new war zone had to come from California. Whether the troops came from the East or California, the Indian conflict area was at the extreme end of Union supply lines.

As noted earlier, some problems in Civil War Western defense were associated with greater reliance upon state and civilian authority in the wartime West. State and territorial volunteer regiments were as or more answerable to their governors than to the president and U.S. Army authorities. Unfortunately for the Indians, these governors were often more concerned about their political futures than with maintaining good relations with the Indians or prosecuting warfare against the appropriate Indians. The most obvious example is Colorado territorial governor John Evans. In 1864, Evans gave those southern Cheyenne who would cease hostilities an ambiguous offer of amnesty. At the same time, he essentially gave a free hand to the fanatical but politically powerful director of the Military District of Colorado, John M. Chivington. The result was the Sand Creek Massacre. A House of Representatives investigation would later conclude that Evans' "prevarication and shuffling" had played a large role in the tragedy.

The situation in Confederate Texas, however, was far worse than in Union states. Two completely separate forces defended Texas against Comanche and Kiowa raids. Confederate military officials directed such mobile organizations as the Frontier Cavalry Regiment and Bourland's Texas Cavalry Regiment. The governor of Texas, meanwhile, commanded a total of nine regiments and five battalions of locally based militia. The state organizations were almost always understrength and inefficient, and they diverted manpower from the more effective Confederate regiments that were also recruited in the state. The two efforts often were not complementary. Two of the worst disasters in the history of the Indian Wars in Texas—the Elm Creek Comanche-Kiowa raid, and the defeat at the Battle of Dove Creek—were partially due to a lack of wartime coordination among the state's defenders.

The withdrawal of Federal troops and the diminution of centralized authority in the West was accompanied by disruptions and suspensions in United States treaty obligations. There were a variety of reasons for the suspensions, including political confusion, the traditionally miserly and arbitrary nature of Congress, the financial demands of warfare in the East, and the loss of southern mail routes. Interestingly, Confederate treaties with the Indians always stipulated that the United States was responsible for annuity payments to Indians allied with the Confederacy. Few Indians understood or cared about why the promised funds and goods were not sent. The United States government failed to grasp what variously promised payments, rations, and trade goods meant to the Indians. Many Plains groups felt that treaty obligations represented a quid pro quo: they accepted the disruption of their hunting caused by white overland emigration and were in turn to be compensated. The loss of such compensation meant that wagon trains and way stations became fair game. For some Western reservation Indians, the suspension of annuities due for the loss of previous territory were viewed as the final and most treacherous in a series of shady dealings by whites. The government also failed to realize the degree to which many Western Indians had grown dependent upon treaty obligations as their traditional means of sustenance eroded away. For these Indians, the suspensions meant starvation; if they faced extinction, what did they have to lose by going to war? The most obvious and tragic example of the last case is that of the Dakotas, whose war is briefly described below.

Fresh demands upon Indian land and resources were the final factor in the encouragement of 1861-1865 Indian conflicts in the West. In 1861 and early 1862, the withdrawal of Regular troops and the focus of white concentration upon the East reduced the use of the overland trails through Plains Indian territory. After that several events coincided to produce even greater pressure upon some Indian groups. This trend perhaps began with the two Confederate expeditions into New Mexico Territory in 1861 and 1862 and with the Union counteroffensive that followed. These are described below. These campaigns restored some use of the stage route through Apache country. Later, the need for Nevada and California silver and gold to finance the Union war effort increased the use of other southern freight routes.

The lust for gold also increased traffic to and through Colorado, Idaho, and Montana. By 1864, continuing yields from the Cherry Creek gold fields near Denver once again tempted prospectors to trespass across Southern Cheyenne and Southern Arapaho hunting grounds. It was not a coincidence that the Cheyenne-Arapaho War began shortly after the restoration of this traffic. The same year, 1864, traders and prospectors cut and began using the Bozeman Trail to the Montana gold fields. This violated the Powder River country, which was by treaty the domain of the Lakotas and Northern Cheyenne. A full-scale war resulted in 1866, when the "Bozeman Trail War" or "Red Cloud's War" began. However, events during the Civil War very much helped bring about later wars with the Lakotas. Unfortunately, as noted above, the new prospectors of 1861-1865 were precisely the sort of individuals who did not belong in potentially explosive areas.

One additional complicating factor in Civil War-era Indian wars merits mention: whites in 1861-1865 often made war on the wrong people. Many did not realize that there were identifiable divisions among Indian peoples, and they could not distinguish among them. This problem constantly complicated military and civilian efforts to carry out campaigning and peacemaking. It is difficult even today to understand the Indian conflicts of the Civil War period without clearly distinguishing among the groups that were at war. For this reason, some specific Indian groups at war in 1861-1865 are identified below. It should be noted that there is often disagreement among anthropologists, linguists, and tribal authorities regarding the terminology and classifications employed in this essay. The term "band" is used in a confusing variety of ways by authors writing of American Indian groups. This is particularly true when discussing the Apaches. Further, the use of the term "tribe" is misleading when applied to the social and political organization of historic Western Indians. Most western groups did not have anything technically approaching a "tribal" system until they produced artificial versions of that form to meet the conditions of the 1934 Indian Reorganization Act.

A. *The Apaches* (Apache name: *Diné* or *Tin-ne-áh*). At the time of the Civil War, there were perhaps 6,000 to 8,000 Apaches, not including 200-400 "Kiowa-Apaches." They occupied an area from westernmost Texas to eastern New Mexico in the United States, and in northern Sonora and Chihuahua states in Mexico. Most of the Apaches lived on terrain that could support only a limited and scattered population, a factor which encouraged diversity among them. Given the broad geographical range and diverse nature of Apache groups, it is not surprising that Apaches were engaged in a wide variety of relationships with citizens of the United States during the Civil War, from invaluable alliances to bitter enmities.

The divisions of the Apaches fell into two major groupings or categories, each grouping distinguished by differences in language, location, and subsistence base. Apaches in the eastern grouping roamed more open country and were more greatly influenced by contact with Plains tribes. For these reasons, the divisions in this grouping are sometimes termed "Plains Apaches." At the same time, it is fairly easy to distinguish between the divisions of the eastern grouping of Apaches. Apaches in the western grouping frequently lived in or near mountain ranges and escarpments, where they could take refuge from rival Indian peoples and Mexicans. The divisions among the western grouping of Apaches were often defined by non-Apaches and are somewhat artificial. The divisions described below remained fairly constant throughout the nineteenth century and were the closest form of organization to what might, with inaccuracy, be called Apache "tribes." However, the creation of Apache reservations and agencies following the Civil War caused major disruption and realignment in the identity of the subdivisions or bands.

1. *The Jicarilla division, eastern grouping.* This division was located in the northeastern portion of current New Mexico, with members often spread among Puebloan peoples. The Jicarilla division of the eastern grouping of Apaches enjoyed the closest relationship with the United States during the Civil War. Most of them had been at peace with the United States since the conclusion of a brief conflict in 1854-1855. Some of its members were recruited by the U.S. Army for service against Plains tribes during the Civil War. The seventy-five Jicarilla and Ute auxiliaries that accompanied Kit Carson's 1864 campaign against the Comanche and Kiowa were considered invaluable to the survival of that expedition.

2. *The Lipan division, eastern grouping.* The northern band of Lipan Apaches was a remnant population that had survived several years of warfare with the state of Texas. Around the time of the Civil War, the northern band was merging with the Mescalero division (below). The southern band of Lipan Apaches lived in the northern part of Coahuila state in Mexico.

3. *The "Kiowa-Apaches"* (Kiowa-Apache name: *Notion Den*), *eastern grouping.* As noted under "Kiowa" below, this unique population spoke Apache but was closely associated with the Kiowa Indians and lived a southern Plains lifestyle.

4. *The Mescalero division and the "Operations Against the Mescaleros" of September 1862-March 1863.* The Mescaleros occupied an area from the south central part of current New Mexico south to the Bend area of the Rio Grande basin in Texas. Opinion is split as to whether to consider the Mescalero division part of the eastern or western grouping of Apaches. The Mescalaro division can be categorized as eastern or Plains grouping by location, but the bands within it were often associated with the eastern Chiricahua band within the western grouping.

In the summer of 1862, the Mescaleros became the first Western Indians to initiate serious hostilities. This division of Apaches had generally been at peace with the United States following a series of military operations in 1855, though the army did launch a brief punitive operation against them two months before the onset of the Civil War. The two major bulwarks against the Mescaleros were Fort Stanton, New Mexico Territory, and Fort Davis, Texas. Unlike some other installations, these forts were located in the very midst of the Indians they were intended to control. As long as the two positions were held, they remained powerful symbols of white commitment to thwarting Mescalero raiding. However, Forts Stanton and Davis were abandoned by the U.S. Army in April of 1861. That July, the Second Texas Mounted Rifles reoccupied Fort Davis in anticipation of an invasion of Union-held New Mexico. Shortly before this, Lt. Col. John R. Baylor believed he had secured good relations with a Mescalero group in the Davis Mountains under Chief Nicholás. However, in August the Apaches raided the post for horses. When a fourteen-man detachment from Fort Davis pursued, Nicholás ambushed the party in a canyon and annihilated it. The Confederates decided to abandon the New Mexico Campaign in May of 1862. Just before the final troop withdrawals in the late summer of 1862, they carried out an unsuccessful operation against the Mescaleros from Fort Stanton. The subsequent Confederate withdrawal into Texas left Fort Davis empty.

The Mescaleros had now seen both the United States and the Confederacy evacuate the two forts built to control them. Triumphantly, the Apaches burned both facilities and launched a series of raids against ranches and settlements in New Mexico and western Texas. When the Federals reoccupied New Mexico Territory, Brig. Gen. James H. Carleton took over the the territorial military department. In September 1862, Carleton issued a notorious order that "all Indian men of the [Mescalero] tribe are to be killed whenever and wherever you can find them." He also ordered Lt. Col. Christopher "Kit" Carson's First New Mexico Cavalry regiment to reoccupy Fort Stanton and sent two punitive columns into the field. The operations also involved the First California Cavalry and, unusually for the Civil War period, one Regular U.S. Army regiment, the Fifth Infantry.

The 1863 Federal Mescalero operations in New Mexico did not result in so much as an intense skirmish. Perhaps the most memorable event took place when one of Carleton and Carson's subordinates took Carleton's order literally and slaughtered two sub-band chiefs and their followers while entertaining them at a parlay. (Another of Carleton's officers commanded the troops that murdered Mangas Colorado of the Chiricahua Apaches under similar circumstances.) Despite the lack of fighting, 400 harried Mescaleros were soon driven into confinement onto the Bosque Redondo Reservation in eastern New Mexico Territory, where they were joined by the defeated Navajos in 1864. By 1865, all of the Mescaleros had slipped off the uninhabitable reservation, and by then there was little inclination to force them to return. The United States Army was unable to strike another serious blow unable to strike another serious blow to the Mescaleros until 1867, and warfare with them continued into the late 1870s.

5. *The Chiricahua division and the "Cochise's War" phase of the Apache Wars, February 1861-October 1872*. The bands of this division was located in what are now southwestern New Mexico and southeastern Arizona. There were at least three bands or subdivisions of Chiricahuas during the Civil War. The Southern Chiricahua band (Apache name: *Nednhi*) was known variously during the Civil War as the Carrizaleños, Janeros, or Pinery Apache band. Most of the Southern Chiricahua range was in the northeastern corner of Sonora and the northwestern corner of Chirihuahua states, Mexico. Many of this band's members were joining other bands by the time of the Civil War because of a decline in their numbers as a result of Mexican military campaigns. The Central Chiricahua band (Apache name: *Chihenne*) was usually known during the Civil War as the Gila Apaches. The eastern and central bands were not distinct culturally or linguistically. The Eastern Chiricahua band (Apache name: *Chihenne*) was usually known during the Civil War as the Gila Apaches. This band lived in the mountains and along the rivers of modern-day southwestern New Mexico. The Eastern Chiricahua sub-bands included the Copper Mines, Mimbres, Mogollon, and Ojo Caliente or Warm Springs Apaches. A fourth division, a small northern band known to other Apaches as the *Bedonkohe*, broke up during the Civil War, and its members joined either the eastern or central Chiricahua bands. The Cochise's War" phase (1861-1872) of the Apache wars was fought primarily by the central and eastern bands of the Chirichauas.

Most members of the Chiricahua disision of Apaches avoided hostilities with United States citizens prior to the Civil War. Mexico was considered a more vulnerable and deserving target for raids and retaliations, and the Apaches had no desire to face two enemies at the same time. However, this situation changed dramatically two months before the outbreak of the Civil War.

By most accounts, the treatment of Cochise in the "Bascom Affair" was the reason for the transformation. Cochise [Apache *Cheis*] was one of the most respected leaders of the central or Chekonen Chiricahuas. In early 1861, Cochise and a handful of followers were living in a canyon at the south end of the Dos Cabeza Mountains, near the Apache Pass mail station. On February 4, 1861, a young lieutenant named George N. Bascom confronted Cochise and accused him of stealing stock from a ranch eighty miles west, and of kidnapping

Cochise,
a member of the
Chiricahua Apache.

Online Database

the stepson of the ranch owner. Cochise countered that the raid had probably been carried out by one of the western bands of Apaches. Bascom attempted to seize Cochise and the six relatives and companions with him as hostages. Cochise slit the wall of Bascom's tent with his knife and escaped (an incident which explains why the Apaches called this the "cut-the-tent" affair). Two days later the Apaches began seizing mail and freight train employees in the pass as hostages. Cochise offered to exchange his hostages along with some captured mules for Bascom's hostages, but Bascom insisted that the rancher's stepson be returned. Cochise did not have the boy and was thus unable to comply.

Both sides spent the next two weeks attempting to ambush one another, capture more hostages, and gather supporters. Bascom sent couriers for reinforcements and received two companies of mounted troops from Fort Buchanan to the west. At this the Apaches abandoned the area of the pass and left the mutilated bodies of their hostages at its summits. Bascom, in turn, executed his hostages, including Cochise's brother and two nephews. Cochise spent almost a decade retaliating against United States citizens. He was joined in this by his father-in-law Mangas Colorado [*Dasoda-hae*], leader of a Mimbres group of eastern or Chinenne Apaches. Mangas Colorado was eventually murdered by guards while attempting to negotiate a peace settlement at the beginning of 1863.

During the five months following the Bascom Affair, a punitive action against the Chiricahuas came to nothing, and Cochise, Mangas, and their associates struck blows as least seven times against wagon trains, military detachments, and small communities. In May of 1862, the "California Column" of 2,350 recruits arrived in the Arizona portion of New Mexico Territory. Its purpose was to reinforce the 1862 Union counteroffensive against Confederates holding the Rio Grande valley. However, the approach of the troops was enough to convince the Confederates that they did not have the resources to hold the territory. James H. Carleton, the column's commander, resolved to reestablish a military presence in southern Arizona and to reopen communications between California and the towns on the Rio Grande in New Mexico. The route involved was the San Diego—San Antonio state road through Chiricahua country via Apache pass. A scouting party from the column soon met with Cochise and assured him that the Apaches were not the object of their operations. The distrustful Cochise, however, resolved to ambush the next group of soldiers he found.

At noon on July 15, 1862, an advance party of 126 men of the First California Cavalry under Capt. Thomas H. Roberts entered the pass. Cochise's warriors sprang their ambush. The soldiers quickly responded and pulled back to protect their supply train. A "jackass battery" of two mountain howitzers held the Chiricahuas back. However, when the soldiers tried to advance to Apache Spring for water, they were met with a withering fire from brush, ravines, and two Indian breastworks. Roberts deployed skirmishes onto the slopes and had the Apache positions shelled by the howitzers. By 4:00 p.m. the Apaches had retreated. The fight was almost exactly repeated the next day, down to a struggle for the spring, but the advance managed to proceed eastwards thereafter. One trooper was killed, and another wounded. Traditional Apache accounts claim that few, if any, Apaches were killed.

Despite the limited losses, the Battle of Apache Pass was significant. It quickly led to the establishment of a major fort, Fort Bowie, adjacent to the pass. In addition, the incident marked another progression towards long term warfare with the Apaches. The "Cochise's War" (1861-1872) phase of the Apache wars would be largely conducted by the central and eastern bands of the Chiricahuas. Members of some of the Chiricahua sub-bands remained through several cycles of hostilities until Geronimo's surrender in 1886. The United States' conflict with the Apaches was, along with the war against the Lakotas, one of the two longest and most expensive Indian wars in the country's history.

6. *The Western Apache Division.* The bands of this division occupied small mountain ranges and river valleys in what is now south central Arizona. Identifiable bands during the Civil War included the Arivaipa, Pinal, San Carlos

[River] or Gileños, and White Mountain or Sierra Blanca Apaches. During the war, the White Mountain band or its eastern sub-band was often called the Coyotero Apache band. Prior to the Civil War and "Cochise's War," the Coyoteros and Pinals were among the bands which most frequently clashed with ranchers and settlers of United States. However, other "Western Apaches" bands remained peaceful until the 1870s. During that decade the latter were finally driven to resistance by mining and ranching inroads, poor reservation conditions, and the massacre and enslavement of a group of Arivaipas in 1871.

B. *Northern California Indians at War, 1861-1864.* Prior to the California Gold Rush of 1848-1850, the many different Indian groups of northern California lived in two different cultural areas. Each region was a varied patchwork of small- to medium-sized territories defined by mountain ranges and major streams. Perhaps no other Indian population in the United States ever suffered more abuse than did that of northern California. Prospectors using the Lassen and other mining trails exposed the Indians to diseases that became epidemics. The state backed Indian hunting expeditions by hostile miners on the grounds that this protected isolated settlers. California also enacted laws in 1850 and 1860 legalizing the enslavement of Indians as a labor force. Would-be reformers finally insisted that the surviving Indians be "protected," and Congress funded five reservations in 1853. Militia and vigilantes began driving the Indians onto these reservations in incidents like the 1857 "Death March" to the Nome Cult Reservation. But instead of protecting the Indians, concentrating them on the reservations exposed them to further assaults. Though the incessant robbery and murder of California Indians received little national attention, the constant kidnapping of young Indians for San Francisco Bay brothels reached the point that the U.S. Commissioner of Indian Affairs complained to the president.

In the spring of 1861, several of the confined groups decided to retaliate. Elements of the Fourth and Sixth U.S. Infantry regiments were dispatched to handle the outbreak. The campaign pitted members of the Hupa, Wintu, Wiyot, and other peoples against the Fourth and Sixth United States infantry regiments in the redwood forests of northern California. Just a few weeks after the first shots were fired in the Civil War, some of the intensely fought Indian battles of the Civil War period were waged. The most costly encounter was on April 14 and 15 at Mad River, where a detachment of thirty-one men of the Sixth Infantry killed twenty-five Indians. In the summer and fall the U.S. Regulars were finally pulled out of California, most to fight in Virginia. A lull in the fighting then occurred, but by winter growing numbers of hungry Indians were slipping off the reservations.

Early in 1862, a state volunteer regiment, the Second California Infantry, took up the pursuit of the off-reservation Indians, but with limited success. In the fall of 1863, a militia unit of miners familiar with the region, the First Battalion California Mountaineers, was unleashed. Supported by elements of the Second and Sixth California regiments, the Mountaineers wore down the Indian band leaders. Three of the major resistance leaders capitulated by the summer of 1864, and the conflict petered out. These resistance leaders would be among the first residents of the military prison on Alcatraz Island in San Francisco Bay. Between the discovery of gold and the end of the unnamed conflict, as much as 75 percent of the state's Indian population had died of "extermination," disease, or starvation.

C. *The Sioux Indians, the Dakota Conflict, and the Dakota Territory Expeditions* (Sioux/Dakota name for the "Sioux": *Oceti Sakowin* or *Otchenti Chakowin*). Up to fifteen identifiable groups have been indiscriminately referred to as "Sioux." These peoples have shared a common language, called "Sioux" by outsiders and Dakota by its users, and they viewed one another as natural allies. Yet, Dakota-speaking Indians have always made distinctions among themselves. By the time Europeans encountered these peoples, its members identified among themselves as the "Seven Council Fires." These *Oceti Sakowin* , as they were called in their own language, formed a loose alliance. As various Dakota-speaking Indians migrated westward in the late 1700s, three broad divisions emerged among the Oceti Sakowin. Each division possessed its own location, subsistence base, and dialect. Today, the three divisions are regarded by many members as three autonomous nations, and these members tend to reject the use of the generic term "Sioux."

1. *The Dakota Nation and the Minnesota Dakota War of 1862.* Members of the Dakota or eastern division of the Sioux Indians were usually called the "Santee Sioux" (from their Dakota name, *Isanti*) during the Civil War. The Dakota Nation was regarded as the primal division of the Sioux-speaking peoples, and for this reason the word "Dakota" was often used to refer to the Sioux language in general. However, the term "Dakota" was also used to refer to the dialect of this specific nation. As the easternmost division, the Dakota

were the only one of three that still maintained an ancestral "woodlands" lifestyle at the time of the Civil War.

Originally the Dakotas roamed most of the area of the Great Lakes states plus the eastern edge of North and South Dakota. They still possessed almost all of the state of Minnesota and much of Iowa at the middle of the 1800s. However, in 1851 the four regional subdivisions or "bands" of the Dakotas were pressured by state officials and traders into relinquishing the vast majority of their territory in exchange for what was supposed to be major financial compensation. The treaty negotiated by the Sisitonewan and Wahpeton bands at Traverse des Sioux, Minnesota, would become known as the "Traders' Treaty" after the Dakotas discovered that $400,000 of the payments due them had been turned over to merchants. None of the traders who claimed that the Indians owed them this money was required to produce any substantiation. The two treaties reduced the Dakota lands to a thin strip of reservation along the Minnesota River in southwest Minnesota plus a bit of the eastern edge of Dakota Territory. The Sisitonewan ("Sisseton") and Wahpeton subdivisions resettled around the Upper Sioux or Yellow Medicine Agency. The Mdewakonton and Wahpetonewan subdivisions relocated to the area of the Lower Sioux or Redwood Agency.

Few Indian peoples ever endured so patiently so long a series of grievances as did the Dakotas. This may explain both the explosive fury with which their war erupted and the complete surprise with which their attacks caught their white neighbors. Over the decade following the treaty negotiations, the Dakotas were frequently exposed to hunger and disease on their inadequate reservations. The Dakotas also found themselves in growing debt to and dependency upon whites. Indian agents and "friends" of the Indians heightened tensions by offering favors to culturally and economically assimilated "farmer Indians" and by speaking in derogatory terms of the "wild" or "blanket" traditional Indians.

Despite the Dakotas' frustrations, there was only a single serious major incident of Dakota violence prior to the Civil War. Inkpaduta was the head of a small group of renegades that had been outlawed for the killing of several legitimate Wahpekute leaders. In 1856 and 1857, Inkpaduta set out to avenge the murder of his brother by a white whiskey dealer. His men killed fifty-seven settlers and kidnapped several women in attacks at Spirit Lake, Iowa, and the nearby Minnesota town of Jackson. The United States government did not feel it necessary to take action as the Dakota leader, Little Crow (*Cetan Wakan*

Mani) attempted to exterminate the outlaws and drove them west, far into present-day North Dakota.

By 1861, however, it was the entire Dakota nation that was angry. A crop failure that summer left the Dakotas in great need of supplies and promised rations. Unfortunately, the coming of the Civil War delayed the annual annuities due the Indians, and no explanation regarding this was sent to the Dakotas, their agents, or reservation traders. The merchants cut off credit, while the Indian agents refused to distribute any rations due until the distribution of the payments. Many Dakotas became convinced that they were being systematically cheated and starved. Resentment began to flame into war when four young Mdewakantons, without much forethought as to the consequences, killed some settlers near Acton, Minnesota. At a rapidly called band council, many of the warriors argued that since all of the Dakotas would likely be punished for the murders, it would be best to launch a preventive strike against white Minnesotans. Little Crow, who was an influential negotiator, believed that a war would turn out disastrously, but did not want to lose his position among the Dakotas. If they were to die, he explained, it would be best to die as warriors.

At daybreak on August 18, 1862, a war party of Mdewakantons and Wahpetonewans attacked, sacked, and burned the Lower Sioux Agency and killed the first twenty whites. Word quickly reached the portion of the Fifth Minnesota occupying nearby Fort Ridgely, and the fort's commander, Capt. John S. Marsh, set out with a detachment. On reaching the Redwood Ferry, which gave access to the agency, the party was ambushed, and Marsh and twenty-three of his men drowned or were shot. When the news reached the Sisitonewan and Wahpeton chiefs around the Upper Agency, many of the men of their bands were forced to take sides. Some felt obligated to support Little Crow's warriors, while others wanted no part of the conflict. John Other Day and several other assimilated Dakotas or mixed parentage Dakotas slipped away from the Upper Agency to warn area whites and escort them to safety. When Little Crow arrived, he found the agency abandoned by its white occupants. The fleeing employees and settlers would be among the first of as many as 40,000 white refugees.

Though Little Crow was the leading figure in the war, he was unable to prevent maurading or to get the Dakota combatants to agree on a single strategic goal. Little Crow pressed for a united and rapidly undertaken attack on Fort Ridgely, but could not bring it about until August 20. By then, the fort was defended by Lt. Timothy J. Sheehan and 180 soldiers and armed civilians. Little Crow and 400 Dakotas attempted to surprise the garrison with an attack from from a northern ravine. The warriors, however, were held back by artillery fire and the soldiers' superior weapons. Two days later, approximately 800 Dakotas attempted two more attacks from other ravines but were again defeated.

Meanwhile, on August 19, a separate group of around 100 Indians attempted to take and sack the town of New Ulm. Refugees from four other communities had increased the town's population to 1,500 people, but only 250 were armed. A state court justice named Charles Flandrau successfully organized house-to-house fighting until a cloudburst ended the attack. On August 23, some of the warriors thwarted at Fort Ridgely participated in a second attack against New Ulm by 650 Dakotas. This time the back and forth fighting centered on a three-block stockaded area. During the two attacks on the town, over forty defenders were killed and 190 structures burned. But with the failure of the disunited attacks at Fort Ridgely and New Ulm, the Dakotas lost the offensive and initiative.

When word of the agency killings reached Governor Alexander Ramsey at St. Paul, he appointed former trader and governor Henry H. Sibley to lead a relief expedition. Sibley and his 1,800 men did not arrive at Fort Ridgely until August 31. Sibley sent a detachment of 170 men ahead to reconnoiter the Lower Sioux Agency and bury the bodies there. On September 2, Little Crow's warriors surrounded and attacked the unprepared and encamped detachment at Birch Coulee. During the siege that developed, the Sixth Minnesota Infantry lost twenty-two men killed, most dying in the initial assault. Sibley rescued the encircled men the next day. From Birch Coulee, Sibley's column continued up the Minnesota River. On September 23, the command was encamped on Lone Tree Lake. Little Crow planned to ambush Sibley's force while the troopers were in motion on the narrow government road along the valley, but a foraging party stumbled into his concealed warriors. During the engagement that followed, some thirty warriors were killed, including the second most prominent Dakota leader, Mankato. Because the Dakota forces began to break up and disperse, the erroneously named Battle of Wood Lake is considered the decisive engagement of the Dakota Conflict.

Three days after the defeat, the Dakotas released 269 white and mixed-ancestry captives to Sibley. He immediately began recording testimony against their captors. Over 2,000 warriors were eventually imprisoned while awaiting trial, and thousands more were confined to what would later be called concentration camps. Over 300 Dakotas were quickly sentenced to death, but only 38 judged guilty of rape and/or murder were hanged. President Lincoln commuted the sentence of most of the other prisoners on determing that they had been legitimate combatants.

Depending on the speaker's perspective, the Dakota's struggle had been variously known as the "Dakota Conflict," the "Minnesota Uprising," the "Dakota War," or the "Santee Sioux War." Whatever it is termed, it was the costliest Indian war in lives and personal property of any Indian war in United States history. Five hundred to eight hundred settlers were killed. Although the majority of the Dakotas did not join in the fighting, over 20 percent of the 6,500-7,000 Dakotas in Minnesota may have died in the fighting or the immediate retaliation. Little Crow was eventually shot and killed by a farmer in Minnesota a year later while foraging for berries. Most of the Dakota survivors were driven westward and forced either to scatter in small groups across the Northern Plains or join the Nakotas and Lakotas. The Sibley and Sully expeditions that persued them in 1863 and 1864 helped draw the other two "Sioux" nations into war with the United States as well. (See "Lakota Nation" below.) A remnant population of Dakotas survived for decades more in Minnesota by remaining as obscure as possible. In recent years, several Dakota tribal businesses and offices have been established near Morton, Minnesota.

2. *The Nakota Nation.* Speakers of the Nakota dialect were the *Wiciyela* or "middle people" among Dakota language speakers. Their population at the time of the Civil War is uncertain. They occupied much of the central section of the Missouri River and its tributaries, including what is now part of eastern North Dakota and South Dakota. There were two subdivisions of Nakotas. By the time of the Civil War, the Ihanktonwan subdivision was known by whites as the "Yankton Sioux tribe." The Ihanktonwanna subdivision was often called the "Yanktonai Sioux tribe" by whites. There has long been a tendency by outside observers to distinguish between the "Yankton" and "Yanktonai" subdivisions of the Nakota while casually lumping the Dakota together. Today, the use of the Nakota dialect has been almost replaced by the use of the Lakota dialect (see below).

Some Nakotas were probably involved in the siege of Fort Abercrombie in modern-day North Dakota, the only engagement of the "Minnesota Sioux War" outside of Minnesota. The Nakota—or at least the Yankton subdivision—were not substantially drawn into war against the United States until 1864 during the

Sully Campaign in Dakota Territory. However, a detachment of impoverished Yanktons also fought for Sully as auxiliary troops.

3. *The Lakota Nation and Dakota Territory Expeditions of 1863-1864.* The Lakotas ("allies") were known during the Civil War as the *Tintatuwan* by Dakota-speakers and as the "Teton Sioux," "western Sioux," or "prairie Sioux" by those whites who could distinguish them from the Dakotas and Nakotas. The Lakota occupied a huge area of the northern Plains stretching from what is now the western halves of North and South Dakota north to Canada and west into present-day Wyoming and Montana. Though its territory is today much reduced, the Lakota population is so prominent that many people tend to refer to anything "Sioux" as "Lakota." Yet, the Lakota nation began as a single member of the seven *ocetis* or "council fires."

By the 1860s, the Lakota division had grown so large—possibly 16,000 in number—that it had split into seven major subdivisions. These were the 1) Hunkpapa subdivision, possibly the group occasionally referred to as "Cut Heads" by whites during the later 1800s; 2) Itazipco subdivision, commonly known to whites by the French translation "Sans Arcs" ("Without Bows"); 3) Miniconjou subdivision; 4) Oglala subdivision; 5) Oohenunpa subdivision, known to whites by the English translation "Two Kettles"; 6) Sicangu subdivision, usually known to whites by the abbreviated French translation "Brulé" ("Burned"); and 7) Sihasapa subdivision, sometimes known to whites by the English translation "Blackfoot" (not to be confused with members of the Blackfoot confederacy of the northern Rocky Mountains). The Lakotas saw the number of subdivisions as significant—seven was a sacred number to them, and the seven subdivisions were seen as analogous to the ancestral seven ocetis of all Sioux-speakers. The subdivisions often corresponded to different *oyates* or lodge circles when Lakotas encamped together for seasonal ceremonies or hunts.

During the 1850s, there had been frequent difficulty between the Lakotas and the army, often over problems created by traffic on the Oregon Trail near Fort Laramie in present-day Wyoming. This was particularly true in the case of the southern subdivisions, those of the Oglalas and Sicangus ("Brulés"). Matters came to a head in 1855, when a group of Sicangu led by Little Thunder suffered heavy losses during a military expedition led by Brig. Gen. William S. Harney. However, there was little open warfare between the Lakotas and the United States for the next eight years other than occasional raiding of stage stations and corrals during the first two years of the Civil War. The troubled peace ended in 1863 with two punitive campaigns into Dakota Territory.

The expeditions were motivated largely by the demands of white Minnesotans that the army to punish Dakotas who had escaped their state following the Dakota "uprising." In addition, there was fear of a Dakota resurgence or a Dakota alliance with their fellow "Siouxs" to the west. In addition, the army regretted not having pursued the renegade Inkpaduta after his depredations in 1857. Rumors—never proven—that he had had a role in the war in Minnesota renewed the military's desire to deal with him. The Dakota conflict had encouraged the War Department to create the new Department of the Northwest in order to better coordinate military activity on the northern prairies and plains. Major General John Pope, who was banished to Minnesota following his defeat at Second Bull Run in Virginia, took command of the department. Pope drew up plans to entrap the Dakotas who had fled west, hoping his operations would also frighten the Nakotas and Lakotas into not giving the Dakotas assistance and not attacking white settlements in their own territory.

Pope ordered a column under Brig. Gen. Henry H. Sibley to proceed northwest up the Minnesota River with four Minnesota volunteer regiments. Sibley forces were to engage any Indians they encountered while bound for

Devil's Lake in present-day northeastern North Dakota. Devil's Lake was reportedly the point to which Little Crow had fled. A second column was to march north up the Missouri River from Sioux City, Iowa, and prevent any Indians driven westward by Sibley from escaping across the river. If all went

Brigadier General
Henry H. Sibley

Generals in Blue

well, the hostile Indian forces would be crushed between the converging soldiers. Unfortunately for Pope, several things went wrong. The second column was delayed, and its commander was reassigned and replaced by Brig. Gen. Alfred Sully, a man who had experience fighting the Cheyenne before the war. Then, half of Sully's force arrived in Sioux City late. Finally, low water prevented Sully's supply steamboats from proceeding up the Missouri River. These delays prevented the two columns from ever meeting.

Sibley entered Dakota Territory on June 24. A month later he learned that a group of Dakotas had recently departed Devil's Lake. Unknown to Sibley, Little Crow, one of Sibley's primary targets, was heading back to Minnesota. Sibley's scouts found a trail heading west, but it was actually that of Standing Buffalo's Sisitonewan ("Sisseton") Dakotas. This group was peaceful and had been near Devil's Lake hunting buffalo. Sibley dropped off part of his wagons and supplies to increase mobility and raced 1,900 of his men southwest along the trace. Meanwhile, Standing Buffalo's people encountered Inkpaduta's renegade group, which was also hunting buffalo, and had fallen in beside them.

On the afternoon of July 24, 1863, Sibley's scouts spotted an encampment of an estimated 3,000 Indians amid a cluster of prairie salt lakes. The men were ordered to establish a fortified camp, with the edge of a plateau between Sibley's position and that of the Indians. A number of Indians, evidently from Standing Buffalo's group, appeared and attempted to parlay with Sibley's soldiers. Dr. Josiah S. Weiser, surgeon of the First (McPhail's) Minnesota Mounted Rangers Regiment, spoke some Dakota and attempted to translate. As he did so, he was shot by one of Inkpaduta's uncontrollable followers. A fight quickly broke out between the soldiers present and some Dakotas concealed in an adjacent ravine on the plateau slope. Sibley ordered the Sixth and Seventh Minnesota infantry regiments to outflank the ravine from the east. He then gave instructions for his howitzer crews to advance and shell the ravine from the high ground being ascended by the infantry. A useful knoll on the plateau provided the battle its name, Big Mound. Meanwhile, McPhail's rangers made a wide swing to the west to prevent any Dakotas from descending the plateau crest and escaping. The engagement became a running battle, with the outnumbered warriors falling back in clusters and trying to create sufficient delay for their families to break camp. The battle was the most hotly contested one in six days of fighting.

McPhail's rangers pursued the Indians for fourteen miles through the chain of lakes. Finally, the fleeing Dakotas and Sisitonewans were able to disperse

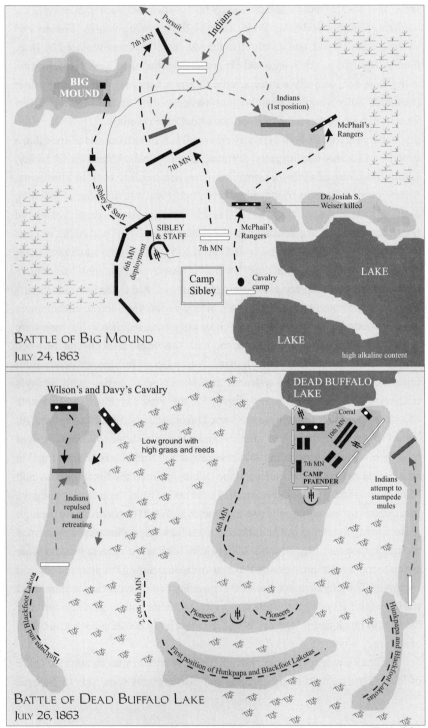

BATTLE OF BIG MOUND
JULY 24, 1863

BATTLE OF DEAD BUFFALO LAKE
JULY 26, 1863

Theodore P. Savas

and escape under cover of darkness. On July 26, Sibley's column retraced the troopers' route. The Sisitonewan Lakotas had by now fled elsewhere. However, Inkpaduta had just managed to form a temporary union with a group of Hunkpapa and Sihasapa ("Blackfoot") Lakotas who were hunting in the area. Skirmishing broke out near the lake where the pursuit had ended two days earlier. A bison carcass seen there would later provide the name of the second engagement, the "Battle of Dead Buffalo Lake." At first, the opposing sides simply fired upon one another at long range. The only serious battling occurred when a party of Indians attempted to work their way around the east side of the Minnesotans' camp and stampede their mules. Afterwards the Dakotas and Lakotas withdrew.

Sibley was determined to pursue the quickly retreating Indians, but after a twenty-one mile march to Stony Lake his men and animals were exhausted. When the column attempted to resume the march on July 27, the lead regiment collided head-on with a massed charge by the Indians. Only the Minnesotans' superior firepower saved them. The Dakotas and Lakotas spent several hours probing for weaknesses in Sibley's lines but could find none, nor could they capture his supply wagons. Sibley pursued the Indians westward as far as the Missouri River. There were a number of brief encounters while the Dakotas and Lakotas successfully covered the crossing of their families. Sibley waited three days for the arrival of Sully's column, then returned to Minnesota. He later reported that he had killed a total of 150 Indians in the three major battles; the Lakotas and Dakotas maintained that they had lost only 24 men.

Because of the July delays, Sully did not reach the intended rendezvous point until late August. A few captured Indians informed him that some of the groups Sibley had driven across the Missouri River had returned to the east side to continue their hunting. Sully decided to strike at these, even though he could no longer coordinate his operation with Sibley's. The advance of Sully's column drove many of the disparate groups east of the Missouri together for mutual defense. On the afternoon of September 3, scouts reported an encampment which was later judged to contain 300-600 tipi lodges. The perhaps 4,000 people present included Dakota refugees, Ihanktonwan ("Yankton") Nakotas, and Hunkpapa and Sicangu Lakotas.

There was a standoff at the village for three hours while the scouts reconnoitered it and Indian elders attempted to negotiate with the scout battalion. Meanwhile, Sully was approaching with most of the 1,800 men of the Sixth and Seventh Iowa and Second Nebraska cavalry regiments. When the

Indians spotted Sully's force, the Indians broke camp and fled. Sibley ordered the Second Nebraska to cut off any retreat southward. A detachment of Iowans was sent to seize Whitestone Hill, which lay across a potential escape route to the south. Other Iowans charged through the village, taking prisoners as they did so. Many of the Indians turned east and attempted to escape through a ravine but were trapped there by more of Sully's troops. Sully ordered his soldiers to begin shooting into the ravine, eager to cut off any escape that might take place under the cover of approaching darkness. The firing was so intense and was conducted so blindly that some of Sully's soldiers shot other soldiers.

The Battle of Whitestone Hill was the most costly battle between whites and Sioux-speaking Indian in the years 1862-1864. Estimates of the Indian dead range from 100 to 300. Sully claimed that most of the casualties were warriors, but many of those killed in the ravine probably were women, old men, and children. The soldiers also captured 165-200 prisoners, mostly women and children. Most of the Indians' camp equipment and the meat drying for the winter were destroyed. During the battle and two subsequent days of fighting, the Nebraskans and Iowans lost twenty-two men killed and fifty wounded. Most of the casualties occurred during a brief Indian counterattack at the ravine and during an Indian attack on a cavalry search operation on September 5.

Sully's column withdrew to the Missouri River valley, where it encamped in present-day South Dakota during the winter of 1863-1864. General Pope, meanwhile, formed a plan for permanently "pacifying" the Dakota Territory. Sully would be reinforced with a small brigade of volunteers marched cross country from Minnesota, increasing his command to 2,200 men. The main column and infantry regiments to follow would establish forts at positions along the Missouri River and its tributaries. Sully's two brigades rendezvoused on June 30, 1864. After marching into North Dakota, Sully established a location for Fort Rice. Many Lakotas interpreted this as a hostile act and several times seemed to be contemplating an attack on the position. On July 9, Sully learned that a number of Indian groups were traveling northward, concentrating in the Badlands country of the Little Missouri River basin. Many of the Indians were Lakotas who had not been involved in the fighting in 1863. Sully promptly ordered his troops on a 400-mile march west to confront the Indians.

On the morning of July 28, Sully's scouts located a camp of an estimated 1,600-1,800 tipis near the base of Kildeer (Tahkahokuty) Mountain. Elders met with Sully four miles from the village and were in a parlay with him when firing from an unidentified source began. Sully advanced his regiments in a formation unusual for the Civil War era—a Napoleonic hollow square. The Lakotas repeatedly tried to outflank the advancing lines but were driven back each time by rifle fire and artillery. When it became evident that afternoon that there would be no sustained attacks, Sully ordered his men to begin encircling the villages. Field batteries raked the lodges, and the villagers fled by way of the ravines on the slopes of the mountain. Their retreat was covered by a handful of persistent warriors. Major Alfred Brackett's battalion made a successful saber charge against these determined men, but by then many of their family members had successfully escaped. The following morning, Sully left a detachment to destroy the village while the main force attempted to proceed around Kildeer Mountain and cut off the Indians' retreat. However, the rough terrain hampered the pursuit. The soldiers took 156 prisoners, and Sully claimed they had killed 150-300 warriors. Far more seriously for the Indians, the tipis and over 400,000 pounds of bison meat needed for the winter were destroyed.

The consequences of the Dakota Territory expeditions are hard to gauge. The most concrete result was that the army occupied another 450 miles of the Missouri River valley running throughout the current states of North and South Dakotas. Although the Indians had not experienced any crushing blows, Pope and his successor hoped that their five defeats and the presence of two new forts would ensure peace. In October 1865, nine treaties were negotiated with elements of Nakota and Lakota bands. However, the Sibley and Sully expeditions may well have made future warfare more, rather than less, likely. The treaties were signed primarily by "peace chiefs" with limited influence. Sully's two expeditions earned the United States the lasting enmity of many other Lakotas, including the warrior and shaman Sitting Bull (Tatanka Iyotanka), who would inspire the destruction of much of George Custer's command twelve years later at the Little Bighorn.

After the Sibley and Sully campaigns, the Sicangu and Oglala Lakotas resumed their deferred skirmishing with the U.S. Army around Fort Laramie at the beginning of 1865. Some of this fighting was coincident with the Cheyenne and Arapaho attacks on Julesburg, Colorado, to the southeast. The U.S. Regular Army returned to man its Oregon Trail posts at the end of the Civil War. Thereafter, troops were dispatched to build and garrison three forts on the new Bozeman Trail prospectors' route to Montana as well. Still more soldiers garrisoned forts like Fort Rice, providing white travelers more security on the Missouri River. The river soon became a major thoroughfare for gold seekers bound for the Dakota, Montana, and Idaho territories. The incessant violations of Lakota territory that resulted on the routes guaranteed conflict with that nation. Beginning in the late summer of 1866, the Lakotas initiated massive resistance among the peoples of the Northern Plains. They and their allies would remain at war with the army on and off until 1877. Viewed as a whole, the series of "Sioux" conflicts beginning during the Civil War were one of the longest, and in scale the largest, of United States Indian wars.

D. *The Shoshones and the Connor Expedition* (alternate Shoshone names: *Shoshoni, Soshonie*). The Shoshones were a mountain and Great Basin people whose original range had been much reduced during wars with other Indian peoples. At the time of the Civil War, there were three loosely defined geographical divisions of Shoshones. The northern Shoshones and closely associated Bannocks occupied the upper watershed of the Salmon and Snake rivers, largely in present-day central and southern Idaho. The western Shoshones roamed the Great Basin of much of current Nevada and western Utah. The last of these three divisions, the eastern Shoshones (who would become known as the "Washakie Band") were wrestling for control of what is now western Wyoming with the Crows (*Absaroka*) during the period of the Civil War. Shoshone territory overlapped with that of the linguistically related Bannocks, Paiutes, and Utes, and there was considerable intermarriage between these peoples.

The single major encounter between soldiers of the United States and Shoshones involved the 450 people of Bear Hunter (Wairasuap) and Sagwitch's band in the Cache Valley. This was a broad drainage in northeastern Utah Territory and southern Idaho Territory. During the Civil War, tensions were high between Shoshones on one side and prospectors and other travelers passing through Utah on the other side. The new (1862) Montana Trail to the gold fields of Montana Territory ran from Salt Lake City though Bear Hunter's territory. The Overland Stage road through Salt Lake City to the south depleted the grazing of other Shoshone bands. There was occasionally isolated shooting between travelers and Indians on these routes.

In late 1861, the Third California Infantry and the Second California Cavalry regiments were stationed at Camp Floyd near Salt Lake City in order to guard the Overland mail route. This was a serious disappointment to Col. Patrick Edward Connor and his men. Connor had organized the Third California Volunteer Infantry to fight in battles in the Eastern Theater, but instead it had been dispatched to Utah. The next fall, however, it appeared as if the Californians might have an opportunity for heroics after all. After four Shoshones were killed in an incident involving a report of a missing child, Shoshones killed ten prospectors on the Montana Trail. As a result, Connor decided to launch a punitive expedition. On January 21, 1863, he set out with 70 infantrymen and 220 cavalrymen on a 140-mile march north from Salt Lake City. The cavalry advance reached Bear Hunter and Sagwitch's winter encampment on Bear River shortly after dawn on January 29. On seeing the sheer banks and thick willow stands along the river, scouts mistook them for fortifications. The supposed existence of such "breastworks" was later presented as evidence of the Indians' warlike intent.

Major Edward McGarry was ordered to cross Bear River, swing wide with his cavalry around the village, and cut off escape via a gap between the ridges in back of the camp. Once the horsemen were in place, the infantry would launch a frontal assault across the river. The water proved too deep to wade on foot, and some of the riders had to stop and help the infantry across. As they did so, Shoshone warriors opened fire from the willow banks and attempted to purchase time for the women and children to escape. Once the cavalry was across, the troopers rode uphill to the gap made by what is today known as Battle Creek. From the slopes, they began firing down upon the Shoshones attempting to flee in that direction. Once the Indians were trapped between the high ground and the river, the Californians began to pour fire into the village. According to the best estimate, 250 to 275 Shoshones were killed. In addition, around 160 women and children were captured, though they were released the next day. However, according to several area settlers, several women were killed while resisting sexual assault. Only twenty-one soldiers were killed, most during the contested river crossing. Connor believed he won a glorious victory and achieved peace on the Montana Trail and Overland Stage route. His critics, however, argue that he brought on an unnecessary battle with an unjustifiably high loss of lives among the non-combatants.

The survivors of Bear Hunter and Sagwitch's people dispersed, and their descendants are today spread among four federally recognized tribes. The harshness with which Connor had treated the village at Bear River convinced many bands of Shoshones and their relatives, the Paiutes and Utes, that they would have to treat with the United States and try for favorable terms. Some bands did better at this than others. Government commissioners were determined to relocate all groups living astride major trails or holding high quality grazing land like the Cache Valley. In the second Treaty of Fort Bridger in 1868, the Shoshones lost that watershed. However, the battle at Bear River strengthened the position of the Shoshone leader Washakie. His reputation as a friend to whites and his considerable diplomatic skills helped him achieve a relatively favorable treaty for the Shoshones in present-day Wyoming.

The engagement at Bear River set several precedents. It was the first of the five incidents in Western Indian warfare that are most frequently considered massacres. When Col. John M. Chivington led the slaughter of Black Kettle's Cheyennes at Sand Creek in 1864, he was following what he believed to be the example of his mentor, Colonel Connor. Bear River also marked the first time that the U.S. Army deliberately attacked a village in winter when the Indians could not easily escape. This tactic was later used successfully in the Southern Plains Campaign of 1868-1869 and the Red River War of 1874-1875.

E. *The Navajos and the Navajo War of 1863-1864* (Navajo name: *Dine*). At the time of the Civil War, there were perhaps 12,000 Navajos. The fragile natural environment of the Navajo, like that of their linguistic relatives the Apache, could not support a dense population, so the Navajo were a much dispersed people. They were spread out over a vast territory, including the northeastern quarter of Arizona Territory, the northwestern quarter of New Mexico Territory, and the southwestern edge of Colorado. Small groups in the same locale frequently identified themselves as part of the same band and would often recognize the leadership ability of the same headman. However, headmen had little or no control over the actions of individuals, particularly the young men.

Existence in their arid region was often difficult, and many Navajo relied on kidnapping and stealing stock from ranches as a means of obtaining food and labor. Unlike some other Indian peoples, the Navajo viewed raiding as basically an economic activity. Despite this, they had a reputation in the 1860s as one of the most warlike peoples in North America. Some indication of the United States' apprehension about the Navajo is indicated by the fact that they were the only Western Indians always confronted by U.S. Regular troops, as well as state volunteers, throughout the Civil War.

Neither the Mexican or United States governments understood the localized nature or individualism of the Navajo. Individual bands that had not made treaties did not feel bound to abstain from raiding, and thus whites concluded that all Navajo were treacherous. For their part, when whites sometimes retaliated against the wrong bands, Navajo concluded that all whites

Kit Carson

National Archives

were hostile. There was also mutual misunderstanding about the nature of treaties. Whites felt that the purpose of treaties was to create peace between themselves and the Navajo. The Navajo, however, often signed treaties believing that this would gain them assistance against their many enemies.

Sharp fighting broke out between soldiers and Navajo in 1858. In 1860, as many as 2,000 warriors took part in a major attack against Fort Defiance, in what is today northeastern Arizona. The army replied with a concerted and seemingly successful effort to subdue the Navajo in the winter of 1860-1861. The campaign had an unforeseen effect and left the Navajo destitute and easier prey for rustling and slaving parties of Pueblo and Ute Indians, or Anglo and Hispanic settlers. When most of the professional army was withdrawn from the Western forts in 1861, the Navajo were eager and able to resume raiding. They were also embittered by a sense that the United States was intent on punishing their actions, but would not protect them from similar actions by other peoples.

By the end of 1861, James H. Carleton of the Federal Department of New Mexico resolved to either exterminate the Navajo or exile them far from white settlements. However, Carleton's forces were first committed to dealing with the Mescalero Apache and with a Confederate army in New Mexico. As a result, Carleton was not able to turn his attention to the Navajo issue until the middle of 1863. He designated a forty square mile tract in the desert of eastern New Mexico as a Navajo and Mescalero reservation. The reserve was poetically named "Bosque Redondo," Spanish for "round grove of trees." The title was wholly inappropriate, for other than a few cottonwoods near a new fort, there was little else that did or could grow on the desolate land. Carleton used every means possible to get word to the Navajo that unless they went to the reservation they would be killed.

Part of Carleton's plan involved using Kit Carson and his force of 400 men, many from his First New Mexico Cavalry Regiment, and 200 Muwache Ute auxiliaries, to subdue the Navajo. Operating out of the newly constructed Fort Wingate in present-day western New Mexico, Carson's men spent July through November of 1863 destroying the crops and seizing the sheep of Navajo bands. Actual fighting was limited, but the Navajo responded several times by launching raids on the volunteers' horse herds. Winter brought starvation, and handfuls of Navajos began surrendering. Carleton wanted a still stronger show of force and ordered Carson to invade the mysterious Canyon de Chelly in northeastern Arizona.

The deeply entrenched canyon was, in legend, a major refuge and natural fortress for the Navajo people. Carson set out on January 6, 1864. He soon split his command. Captain Albert Pfeiffer's detachment proceeded to the east end or head of Canyon de Chelly. Carson and the majority of the troops marched to the west end or mouth of the defile. Unknown to Carson, Pfeiffer lost his way while proceeding over unfamiliar terrain through falling snow. Instead of arriving at the east end of Canyon de Chelly, Pfeiffer on January 11 arrived at the north end of its major tributary, Canyon del Muerto. When Pfeiffer did not meet him within Canyon de Chelly, Carson carried out a scout from atop the south rim of the canyon. Carson never suspected that Pfeiffer had entered the wrong canyon. Some histories still repeat Carson's misconception as to Pfeiffer's route.

Pfeiffer's command proceeded down Canyon del Muerto over an frozen creek bed. Scattered groups of Navajo attempted to fire down upon him from the rim. The soldiers later commented on the bravery and persistence of an elderly woman who hurled rocks and insults upon them. Pfeiffer finally located Carson near the junction of the two canyons on January 14. Probably no more than fifteen Indians were killed or wounded in the fighting. The action, though, convinced the Navajo that the canyon no longer offered them security. Carson, however, was able to convince a local headman in a parlay that it was safe to surrender to him. It has been suggested that Pfeiffer may have been unwilling to take many prisoners alive, and this may have made submission directly to Carson more attractive. By the time Carson's force was back at Fort Wingate, it was accompanied by over 250 prisoners.

From January through May of 1865, Navajos "came in" in groups as large as 350 persons. In all, some 8,000 Navajos made the "Long March" to the Bosque Redondo Reservation. The journey and the confinement were so devastating that the event is regarded by the Navajos as the watershed event in their history. Parasites from the water of the Pecos River and contagious diseases killed hundreds of them on the reservation. When the Navajos attempted to plant corn and built shelters, army worms killed the crops and the "round grove" was soon exhausted of trees. No one had realized the large size of the Navajo population, and even with thousands of Navajos still in hiding, the army could not supply enough food to those at Bosque Redondo. Even the hardened Carleton became troubled. After four years, the United States relented. In 1868, the War Department designated part of the Navajos' homeland as their reservation, one of the few instances in which and Indian people were restored to an ancestral domain. The wartime experience left the Navajos resolved to remain at peace with whites while committed to maintaining their own traditions. It also encouraged their strong contemporary sense of nationhood.

F. *The Cheyennes and Arapahos and the Cheyenne-Arapaho War of 1864-1866* (Cheyenne name for the Cheyenne: *Tsetschestahase* or *Tsistsistas* ; Arapaho name for the Arapaho: *Inunaina*). By the early 1840s, the Cheyenne were divided into the Northern and Southern Cheyenne. The Northern Cheyenne lived among the Lakota along the North Platte River, particularly in what is now the western edge of Nebraska, much of Wyoming, the southern edge of Montana, and the northern edge of Colorado. An 1854 estimate placed their population at 800 members. The Southern Cheyenne roamed an area south of the Platte River including what is now eastern Colorado, southern Nebraska, most of Kansas, and the northern edge of Oklahoma. Disruptions created by mining and freight traffic across their lands caused a serious decline in the Southern Cheyenne population during the 1850s. For this reason, the number of Southern Cheyenne at the outbreak of the Civil War was probably much lower than the 1854 estimate of 3,200. The assignment of Indian territories by whites in the 1851 Fort Laramie Treaty formalized the distinction between the northern and southern groups. However, despite many decades of separation, the Cheyenne still considered themselves a single people.

The Cheyenne long had close ties with the Arapaho, and the two peoples often placed their lodge circles close together. During the 1850s, the Arapaho also formed two distinct populations, one northern and one southern. This separation was partially also based on preferences for northern Plains versus southern Plains hunting grounds. In addition, some groups preferred Sioux and Northern Cheyenne neighbors while other preferred Southern Cheyenne and Kiowa neighbors. For the most part, the Arapaho territories corresponded to the Cheyenne territories. At the time of the Civil War, there were perhaps 2,500 Arapaho, at least 1,600 of whom were Southern Arapaho. The Southern Arapaho and Southern Cheyenne were assigned a joint reservation in present-day Oklahoma in 1868. Today they share a single tribal government, although there are discussions underway at present regarding a possible separation.

The northern-southern division among the Cheyenne and Arapaho was partially reflected in the differing nature of their conflicts during the Civil War. It would be largely the southern populations that would carry on the Cheyenne-Arapaho War along the Santa Fe and Smoky Hill trails. Meanwhile, the Northern Cheyenne was allied with the Lakota in ongoing efforts to halt traffic through their joint territory via the Oregon and California trails. Also, while the Southern Arapaho and Southern Cheyenne fought side by side against the U.S. Army during the Civil War years, some Northern Arapaho signed on as army scouts.

The U.S. Army had campaigned against the Southern Cheyenne and Arapaho as recently as 1856-1857. In February of 1861, a treaty was negotiated at Fort Wise, Colorado, to present further hostilities. A small number of Cheyenne and Arapaho elders, primarily "peace chiefs," agreed to restrict themselves to an arid tract of land in southeastern Colorado. Most of the Indians were ignorant of the treaty's details, did not believe it committed their particular band, or were confused as to the ill-defined boundaries of the reservation. Colorado's white population, however, felt that any off-reservation Indian was likely hostile.

In the spring of 1864, fighting began with a pointless skirmish during pursuit of some unidentified Indian cattle thieves. During the summer and fall, Southern Cheyenne and Araphos struck at wagon trains, stage stations, and ranches on the emigrant and freight routes running across their traditional territory. The First Colorado and Seventh Iowa cavalry regiments participated in most of the few skirmishes that took place. In August, the governor of Colorado began forming another frontier regiment, the Third Colorado Cavalry. The men in this organization enlisted for only 100 days, determined to win glory for themselves by killing any and all Indians they could before their term ran out.

Several of the peace chiefs, notably the Southern Cheyenne chief Black Kettle (Moketavato) were concerned about their bands being swept up in the turmoil. In August, they met in Denver with Governor John Evans and the commander of the District of Colorado, Col. John M. Chivington. Evans was inclined to take a hard line against all the state's Indians, but issued a vague amnesty to those who would settle for the time being near Fort Lyon in the reservation area. Chivington, however, favored the extermination of the state's Plains Indians under any circumstances. Following the meeting, the post commander directed Black Kettle to Sand Creek, forty miles east of Fort Lyon. His 500 Cheyenne and a handful of Arapaho settled there in a winter encampment believing they were secure.

In November, Chivington led the Third Colorado and part of his old unit, the First Colorado, out of Denver and marched toward Fort Lyon. His target was Black Kettle's camp. Chivington claimed the place harbored "hostiles" and perhaps stolen livestock, and it was one of the few encampments he could readily locate. Chivington picked up additional companies of the First Colorado at the fort, giving him a total of 650-700 men. In spite of the "amnesty" and the presence of an American flag flying over Black Kettle's camp, the Coloradans attacked early on November 29. In the infamous Sand Creek Massacre, at least 150 and possibly as many as 200 Cheyenne and Arapaho were slaughtered. According to most accounts, around two-thirds of the dead were women and children.

Chivington was later soundly condemned for his actions by a congressional investigation. The more immediate consequence, however, was warfare on a dramatically escalated scale. Masses of Southern Cheyenne, Southern Arapaho, and some Oglala and Sicangu Lakota met in council at Cherry Creek in western Kansas to discuss revenge for the Sand Creek killings. They targeted the Colorado community of Julesburg on the Oregon Trails near the Nebraska Territory line. This meant they would also have to deal with the nearby military outpost of Camp Rankin (later renamed Fort Sedgwick). On the morning of January 7, 1865, ten Indian volunteers lured a party of twenty-eight men out of the fort. Several miles south, the Indians ambushed the pursuit, killing over half of the soldiers and accompanying civilians before they could escape. Meanwhile, other attackers rounded up cattle and sacked the hamlet's store and stage company warehouse. The Julesburg-Camp Rankin raid was the "high water mark" of Southern Cheyenne and Southern Arapaho warfare against the United States.

Thus encouraged, the raid's participants made plans to move north to the territory of the Lakota, refugee Dakota (from the Minnesota Dakota conflict), Northern Cheyenne, and Northern Arapaho. There the warriors would attempt to persuade their compatriots to join them on a campaign to sweep the whites from the Plains. To prepare for the winter journey, they raided the South Platte River valley, hitting Julesburg again on February 2. This time the Indians pinned down the defenders of Camp Rankin with gunfire and they burned the community. Troops from Fort Laramie, Wyoming, attempted to bar the way of the Indians as they turned north, but were stymied when two troop detachments had their horses stampeded.

The migrating Indians successfully reached the winter encampments of the Lakota, Northern Cheyenne, and Northern Arapaho in what is now Wyoming. There, they swelled the ranks of the Indians who had defeated the U.S. Army in the Bozeman Trail War of 1866-1867. United States commissioners attempted to negotiate with the remaining Southern Cheyenne and Southern Arapaho, but the Sand Creek Massacre had created too much distrust for peace efforts to succeed. Cycles of mutual retaliation between Southern Cheyennes and Arapahos versus United States citizens continued until the the two Indian nations became the target of the large scale Southern Plains Campaign of 1868-1869.

G. *The Comanche, Kiowa, and the Kiowa-Comanche warfare of 1864* (Comanche name for Comanche: *Nemena*; Kiowa name for Kiowa possibly derived from *Kowtow*). The Comanche homeland was the northwestern third of Texas, but members roamed well into what are now Oklahoma and New Mexico. Several of the divisions of the Comanche were highly mobile and migrated hundreds of miles in the mid-1800s. In addition, the southern Comanche and middle Comanche divisions were being displaced by white settlement from the east and south at the time of the Civil War. For these reasons, it is difficult to determine which divisions of the Comanche were involved in fighting in the Panhandle and upper Brazos River watershed of Texas during the Civil War.

There is scholarly disagreement as to the number of Comanche prior to their settlement on reservations. One widely used estimate puts their mid-nineteenth century numbers at 16,000. However, warfare and pressure from white settlement reduced the population by the time of the Civil War. At the time of the Civil War, there were perhaps six bands or divisions of Comanche. Each was independent of the other except for some kinship ties and, frequently, for cooperation in war. Unusually, even contemporary whites sometimes recognized the divisions among the Comanche, and observers occasionally referred to these as separate "tribes." The Comanche were frequent compatriots of the Kiowa in war, and the Comanche were formally confederated with the Kiowa in the 1867 Treaty of Medicine Lodge Creek. The Comanche did not break this connection until 1963.

1. *Northern Comanches*. The three Northern Comanche divisions roamed the same broad territory as the Kiowa, as far north as Kansas south of the Arkansas River, and as far south as the Red River boundary of Texas. The divisions were 1) Kotsoteka; 2) Quahada or Kwahada division; and 3) Yamparika division. The Yamparika was the northernmost of these bands and the Quahada the southernmost. Many times these divisions wintered or took refuge in the Panhandle region of Texas. Prior to the Civil War, the United States launched several serious campaigns against the northern Comanche divisions from 1858 through the beginning of 1861. A temporary truce of sorts was in effect in the spring of 1861, when Federal Regular troops were withdrawn from the Western frontier posts in order to fight the Civil War in the east. Attacks by Northern Comanche and Kiowa began again in earnest in 1864, and warfare with the northern Cheyenne continued until 1875. The Kotsoteka and Quahada were especially militant, and the latter were among the last Plains Indians to accept settlement on a reservation.

2. *Middle Comanches*. The two middle Comanche divisions were those of the Nokoni and the Tenewa or Tenema. The Middle Comanche were located in northern Texas, in the watersheds up the upper Brazos and Colorado rivers. Their territory overlapped with that of the Quahada northern Comanche, and the Nokoni and Quahada were often allied. The republic (and later, state) of Texas had been at war with the middle and southern Comanche on and off since 1840. Some members of the middle Comanche divisions took advantage of the abandoning of frontier posts during the Civil War to heighten raiding within Texas and try to push back the advancing line of white settlement.

3. *Southern Comanches*. The Southern Comanche consisted of a single division, the Penateka. At the time of the Civil War, the designation "Southern Comanches" was no longer accurate since many members of the Penateka division had been relocated north to the area of the "Wichita and Affiliated

Tribes" Agency in west central Indian Territory [modern Oklahoma] in 1859. There, they signed an alliance with the Confederacy at the beginning of the Civil War. Some Penateka band Comanche may have served as Confederate scouts during the war. However, they do not seem to have participated in the conflict in any appreciable numbers. Once a numerous division, there were as few as 1,000 Penatekas by the time of the Civil War.

4. *Kiowas*. There were approximately 2,000 Kiowa during the Civil War years, including several hundred associated "Kiowa-Apaches." The northern division bands ranged from the Arkansas River in southwestern Kansas to what is today central Oklahoma. The southern division bands ranged from central Oklahoma south to the Red River and occasionally south of that into northern Texas. This differentiation between "northern" and "southern" Kiowa is only geographical and does not reflect any other distinction. Much of the Kiowa's territory overlapped that of the Comanche, and Comanche and Kiowa war parties often rode together. The Kiowa were one of the most aggressive peoples on the Plains, and the United States had actively been at war with them since 1860.

The Kiowa were closely confederated with the so-called "Kiowa-Apaches" (Kiowa-Apache name: *Notion Den*), though the Kiowa-Apaches remained autonomous. The Notion Den were unique in that they spoke Apache but lived largely as other southern Plains peoples. Today, however, the Kiowa-Apaches are officially titled the "Apache Tribe of Oklahoma" (not to be confused with the "Fort Sill Apache Tribe" of Oklahoma, which is descended from Chiricahua Apache prisoners of war).

The Comanche and Kiowa were so aggressive in their prewar raids against more sedentary Indians that the United States' abandonment of Western peacekeeping forts at the beginning of the Civil War encouraged many Indian Territory nations to sign alliances with the Confederacy. In the spring and summer of 1861, Confederate and Texas state officials made peace overtures on behalf of themselves and the Indian Territory Indians. Band chiefs from among four of the five divisions of the central and northern Comanche signed an alliance with the Confederacy at the Wichita Agency in the Leased District of Indian Territory. This signing may well have been done partially to acquire the trade goods promised as annual treaty obligations by Albert Pike, the Confederacy's envoy to Indian Territory.

The Confederacy did not make a concerted effort to enlist Comanche participation in the war. Its aims were simply to produce security on its western frontier. If the treaties gave the Comanche a free hand to attack Union regions, that was well and good. However, the treaties may have served notice to the Comanche that their enemies were not divided against themselves. In addition, the Comanche received a chance to recover from prewar military expeditions. It should also be noted that the Quahadi Comanche and the Kiowa (the groups largely responsible for raids in Texas) did not sign a peace treaty.

After the spring of 1862, the state of Texas was geographically isolated and left on its own to defend two important frontiers. One was a 475-mile boundary running north to south parallel to the "Comanche War Trail" between Indian Territory and Mexico. This frontier was initially defended by the same line of six forts that had been held by the federal government until the war began. The other line was the east-west route of the pre-Civil War mail route, which ran through Mescalero Apache country. Confederate forces were compelled to abandon most of the line through Mescalero territory as the result of a Union counteroffensive in New Mexico Territory in the summer of 1862.

The Confederate powers in Texas, however, made a sustained effort to hold the north-south frontier. The immense gaps between the six posts were guarded by Confederate border regiments recruited in the state, militia companies (sometimes called "minute men"), and citizen posses of "forted up" settlers. Tonkawa refugees from the Indian territory were sometimes employed as scouts at local expense. Even with this effort, the state could not effectively hold the line. In 1864, Kiowa, Comanche, and Kickapoo made increasingly frequent use of the Comanche War Trail and other raiding and migration routes through Texas.

In October 1864, during a raid at Elm Creek in north central Texas, Comanche and Kiowa killed five men at a company outpost held by Bourland's Frontier Cavalry and killed or abducted thirteen civilians from the fortified Fitzgerald Ranch. Many settlers retreated over 150 miles that year to a previous frontier that had been overrun by the tide of white settlement a decade before the war. The United States was forced to install a new line of forts in 1867 to secure the Comanche-Kiowa frontier.

A major revenge for raids like the one at Elm Creek was exacted not by the Confederates, but by their Federal rivals. The Comanches and Kiowas had such a free hand by 1864 that they not only struck Texas ranches and hamlets to the south but wagon trains and way stations along the Santa Fe Trail to the north. James H. Carleton, commander of the Department of New Mexico dispatched Kit Carson in response, as he had sent Carson against the Mescalero Apaches and Navajos. Carson set out from an advance base at Fort Bascom, New Mexico Territory, near the Texas Panhandle, on November 7. His force consisted of 336 men chosen from the experienced First California and First New Mexico cavalry regiments, and seventy-five Muwache Ute and Jicarilla Apache auxiliaries. The column proceeded east with as much stealth as possible into the Comanches' and Kiowas' wintering country. On November 26, 1864, Carson's Indians discovered the village of Kiowa chief Little Mountain on the Canadian River. The advance elements of his column charged through the village while the Apaches and Utes captured the horse herd, which Carson had promised them as booty. The soldiers then proceeded about four miles and discovered the second of what they now realized was a chain of Comanche and Kiowa villages.

At this point, Little Mountain's warriors turned back against Carson's troopers and were soon joined by Indians from the second village. The soldiers held a position on a small knoll adjacent to a trading post ruin known as Adobe Walls. They survived a fight throughout the afternoon largely by lobbing shells from two mountain howitzers into their opponents whenever they massed for an attack. To Carson's disppointment, it was impossible to destoy the second village. Good troop discipline and the confusion created among the Kiowas by the burning of the first village saved Carson's command from disaster as it retreated westward.

All but some Kiowa, Quahadi Comanche, and Nokoni Comanche were forced to settle on a reservation in southwestern [Oklahoma] Indian territory following the war, but many Comanche used the reservation as a refuge from which to resume raiding in Texas. The Kiowa and Comanche warfare continued until the conclusion of the Red River War of 1874-1875.

H. *The Kickapoo versus Texas* (Kickapoo name: *Ki-itaapoa*). The Kickapoo were a diverse, highly mobile people of many autonomous bands. Indeed, their name means "people who move about." At the time of the Civil War, there were three groups of Kickapoo. The largest and most settled group, made up of the Kansas or Prairie bands, lived on a reservation in northeastern Kansas near Fort Leavenworth. Some of the Kansas Kickapoo and their allies, the Potawatomi, enlisted in the Union Second Indian Home Guard Regiment. An Indian Territory group consisted of some Kickapoo who had fled Texas during the Texas-Cherokee War of 1838-1839, when the governor, Mirabeau B. Lamar, sought to drive Indians out of the state. Most of this second group temporarily moved to Kansas during the Civil War as the result of raiding and military foraging in the Indian Territory. The third band, the Texas-Mexico group, remained nomadic and ranged between Kansas and Mexico. This latter group had a reputation for raiding the ranches of Mexican and United States citizens along the Rio Grande valley. Members of the Kansas and Indian Territory groups often joined the migratory group, to which they had marital and clan ties.

In the fall of 1864, many Kickapoo in Kansas decided to migrate to Mexico, largely because the prewar and wartime violence had devastated Kansas (as it had Indian Territory). In addition, Federal officials in Kansas were unable to aid many of the thousands of Indian refugees there. Band leaders Papequah and Nokowhat started out with an exodus of approximately 600 Kickapoo and a handful Potawatomi led by Joseph Bourassa. By New Year's Day 1865, the group had reached Dove Creek. This was a tributary of the Concho River in west Texas, about twenty miles southwest of present-day San Angelo. The chiefs established a camp on the creek for a few days' rest before finishing the journey to the Rio Grande border. Three weeks earlier a scouting party of Texas frontier militia had discovered an abandoned Comanche or Kiowa encampment north of Dove Creek. On finding the trail of the Kickapoo several weeks later, the militiamen assumed that they had found a Comanche war trail.

A militia force of 325 men, led by Capt. N. M. Gillentine, was called out from the Second Frontier District and ordered to rendezvous with 160 men of the Confederate Frontier Battalion under Capt. Henry Fossett. After a delayed juncture, Fossett and Gillentine made plans for an attack at daybreak on January 8. The exhausted militia were ordered to launch a frontal attack across Dove Creek while the Confederates cut off retreat to the south and captured the Indian pony herd. When the shooting began, the Kickapoo took refuge in several overgrown ravines, stood firm, and routed the militia. The Confederate attack from the south was soon pinned down, and the soldiers spent most of the rest of the day defending their positions. The Confederates attempted an orderly retreat as nightfall approached. The Indians raced in, recovered their horses, and pulled several of Fossett's men from their saddles.

The militia and Confederates lost twenty-six men killed and perhaps thirty-five to fifty wounded. These losses were the worst in the history of Texas's Indian warfare. The Kickapoo and Potawatomi lost about a dozen killed. The long term consequences were disastrous for Texas. The Kickapoo interpreted Gillentine's attack as a declaration of war and in the spring began a series of revenge raids. For the next eight years they injured the state at every opportunity. In what was to Texans bitter irony, the Mexican government provided the Kickapoo sanctuary in exchange for their assistance in thwarting Comanche raids. Intense Kickapoo raiding continued until 1873, when Col. Ranald S. Mackenzie led members of the Fourth U.S. Cavalry in a successful punitive expedition across the international boundary. The Battle of Dove Creek partially explains why the Kickapoo today remain a geographically divided nation.

The former Kansas and Indian Territory Kickapoo were eventually settled on a reservation in what is today central Oklahoma. The largest group of Kickapoo lives in northern Mexico on a reservation granted by the Mexican government for the Kickapoo's service in combating Comanche and Apache. However, many of the Mexico Kickapoo continue their ancient practice of moving back and forth across the border with Texas. They are perhaps the last migratory Indians in North America, and are the only persons treated as bi-national citizens by the United States and Mexico.

I. *Western Indian Allies of the U.S. Army. The Pima* (Pima name: *Akimel O'odham*) *and Maricopa.* The Pima were an ancient farming people in what is now south central Arizona. The Maricopa, who lived further north, had moved among them for refuge in the 1840s. In 1862, Maj. Gen. Henry H. Carleton (see above under Mescalero division of Apache) ordered that the Pima and Maricopa be armed against the Apache. From 1863, Pima and Maricopa formed two of the five companies of the militia of the newly formed Arizona Territory.

The Ute (Ute name: *Nutc*). The Ute had been at peace with the United States since 1855, when some southern Ute were defeated militarily. During the Civil War, miners continued to invade the territory of the eastern bands in central Colorado. Meanwhile, Latter Day Saints, or Mormon, settlers continued to occupy the territory of the central Ute and failed to deliver on some annuities promised to end another conflict. War between the Ute and whites was narrowly averted several times. Despite these problems, Union Lt. Col. Kit Carson was able to draw upon his friendship with the Muwache band of Ute of southern Colorado. In 1863, Carson used members of the Muwaches and possibly two other bands of Utes, as well as a few Zunis, as scouts in the Navajo War. In 1864, Muwaches were among the seventy-five men of the Indian auxiliary force that played a major role in Carson's campaign against the Kiowa and Comanche in Texas. (End of Part I; Part II will appear in the next issue.)

Bibliographic Essay

Two published sets of primary sources are essential in researching the role and conflicts of American Indians during the American Civil War. One is the Bible of Civil War scholars, the massive *War of the Rebellion: A Compilation of the Official Records of the Union and Confederate Armies* (Washington, D.C.: U.S. Government Printing Office, 1880-1901). The *Official Records*, commonly known as *OR*, contain most of the battle and campaign reports for the years 1861-1865, including those for Western states. A recent invaluable publication, *The Supplement to the Official Records* (Broadfoot, Wilmington, North Carolina, 1995-ongoing), edited by Janet Hewitt, has published recently discovered reports, letters, and other valuable memoranda, though few to date relate to the Indian Territory or to Indian troops. The other important primary source is the two-volume *Documents of American Indian Diplomacy: Treaties, Agreements, and Conventions, 1775-1979*, edited by Vine Deloria, Jr., and Raymond J. DeMallie (Norman: University of Oklahoma Press, 1999). This new publication contains the text of all wartime Union and Confederate Indian treaties, including those contracted by Albert Pike.

Robert M. Utley's accurate and comprehensive *Frontiersmen in Blue: The United States Army and the Indian, 1848-1865* (Lincoln: University of Nebraska Press, 1981) is with good reason considered the standard military history on Civil War-era Indian wars. Though somewhat cursory at times, *The Civil War in the American West*, by Alvin M. Josephy, Jr. (New York: Alfred Knopf, 1992) makes a good effort to place the Western Indian wars in the larger context of the Civil War. Ray C. Colton's shorter work, *The Civil War in the Western Territories* (Norman: University of Oklahoma Press, 1959), is a good "quick read" that devotes one chapter to the Indian wars of the Civil War years. One of the only secondary sources of information on United States political and military dealings with Indians during the Civil War is David A. Nichols' *Lincoln and the Indians: Civil War Policy and Politics* (Columbia: University of Missouri Press, 1978).

Soldier and Brave: Historic Places Associated with Indian Affairs and the Indian Wars in the Trans-Mississippi West, prepared by the National Park Service, United States Department of the Interior (Washington, D.C.: U.S. Government Printing Office, 1971; out of print) is a concise and balanced source of information on individual battles from the 1840s through 1880s. The Conservation Fund's *The Civil War Battlefield Guide*, 2nd ed. (New York: Houghton Mifflin Company, 1998) is the ultimate compendium of capsule histories of all 1861-65 battles, though only a fraction of the book describes Indian wars battles.

Edwin R. Sweeney's *Cochise: Chiricahua Apache Chief* (Norman: University of Oklahoma Press, 1991) is an excellent and authoritative book that begins with the origins of the Apache wars during the Civil War. There are two easily obtainable works, neither of great depth, on the Dakota Conflict in Minnesota. The longer book, and a highly readable one, is Duane Schultz, *Over the Earth I Come: The Great Sioux Uprising of 1862* (1991; reprint, New York: St. Martin's Press, 1997). *The Sioux Uprising of 1862*, by Kenneth Carley (1961; reprint, St. Paul: Minnesota Historical Society, 1976), is briefer but contains some additional information on military actions. Unfortunately, there has been all too little published on the Sibley and Sully expeditions in present-day North Dakota. *The Shoshoni Frontier and the Bear River Massacre*, by Brigham D. Madsen (Salt Lake City: University of Utah Press, 1985) is the definitive work on the Connor Expedition. It has been criticized for downplaying the Latter Day Saints' role, however inadvertent, in provoking the conflict but helps reveal that the attack at Bear River may have surpassed in inhumanity even the infamous Sand Creek Massacre. Thelma S. Guild and Harvey L. Carter's *Kit Carson: A Pattern for Heroes* (1984; reprint, Lincoln: University of Nebraska Press, 1988) is a popular work on Carson with three brief chapters on the Civil War period that include emphasis on Carson's achievements in the Navajo and Adobe Walls expeditions. As Guild and Carter apparently share some of Carson's confusion about troop locations during the invasion of Canyon de Chelly, some readers may prefer E. O. Clifford's *The Kit Carson Campaign: The Last Great Navajo War* (Norman: University of Oklahoma Press, 1990) on the Navajo War. Guild, Carter, and Clifford all honestly view Carson in a positive light in his dealings with Indians. For a more hard-nosed examination, see *Kit Carson: Indian Fighter or Indian Killer?* (Boulder: University Press, 1996) by R. C. Gordon-McCuthen, ed. Stan Hoig's *The Sand Creek Massacre* (Norman: University of Oklahoma, 1963), has been criticized by some as too sympathetic with the Cheyenne, but it clearly remains the best work on the background of the Cheyenne-Arapaho War of 1864-1866.

A CONVERSATION
WITH BATTLEFIELD INTERPRETER DOUG KELLER

Interviewed by Michael A. Hughes

C harles Douglas Keller has the distinction of being one of the only National Park employees to have interpreted the northern Plains wars, the southern Great Plains wars, and the role of Indians in the American Civil War. This breadth of knowledge is the result of his having been an interpreter at Little Bighorn [formerly Custer] Battlefield National Monument, Bent's Old Fort National Historic Site, and Pea Ridge National Military Park. Keller earned his B.A. in history at the University of Northern Colorado. Former Little Bighorn superintendent James Court has referred to Keller as one of his great "discoveries." Court was impressed with his abilities when Keller visited Little Bighorn on holiday in 1982. Historian and current superintendent Neil Mangum added Keller to the park's staff following that meeting. Keller is currently an interpretive specialist at the Pea Ridge battlefield, where one of the most important Civil War encounters west of the Mississippi River occurred on March 7-8, 1862.

MAH: Pea Ridge is the best known Civil War battle in which Indians participated. How many Indians were present and which Indian units were involved? I know that there is some quibbling about the correct designation of those units.

CDK: Here at the park we refer to the units as the First Cherokee Mounted Rifles, under [Col. John J.] Drew, and the Second Cherokee Mounted Rifles, under Col. Stand Watie. Two other Indian regiments were to have been under Confederate Brig. Gen. Albert Pike's command at the battle, but they were delayed in the Indian Territory waiting for missing treaty payments to arrive. The Choctaw-Chickasaw [Mounted Rifles] Regiment finally marched east into Arkansas, but it was with the absent Confederate supply train during the battle. The men might have been as close as the sound of the guns at Pea Ridge when the fragments of the Cherokee regiments began trickling back.

As for the numbers, Pike reported nearly 1,000 Indian recruits in his after-action report. However, historians William Shea and Earl Hess [see the recommended reading list below] suggest there were only around 800 Indian participants in the fighting. It might be safe to say that there were 800 to 1,000 Indians with Pike at Pea Ridge.

MAH: How did Indian regiments come to be present at Pea Ridge, outside of the Indian Territory?

CDK: That's a complicated story, but I'll put it as briefly as I can. Initially, Cherokee Principal Chief John Ross favored neutrality. He was opposed by his longtime political nemesis Watie, who had been in the minority faction of the tribe that had agreed to the Treaty of New Echota, which led to the selling of the

Cherokees' lands in Georgia and their removal over the "Trail of Tears" to Indian Territory [present-day Oklahoma]. When the Civil War began, several Arkansans, including a Watie relative and an attorney, encouraged Watie to begin raising a Cherokee militia company for the tribe's "defense." This became the core of a Cherokee

John Ross

National Archives

regiment, and Watie was commissioned by the Confederacy as its colonel. Between the raising of this regiment, the allegiance of other tribes with the Confederacy, and a Confederate victory at Wilson's Creek, Missouri, on August 10, 1861, Ross and the neutralists lost credibility within the tribe. These events made it easier for Stand Watie to force the tribes' leaders towards allegiance to the Confederacy. Eventually Ross caved and signed an alliance with the Confederates.

MAH: Did the Indian nations agree to become Confederate allies or Confederate protectorates?

CDK: Technically they were protectorates. You can lay ultimate responsibility for any Indian atrocities at Pea Ridge on [Confederate Army of the West commander] Early Van Dorn. He was out of bounds when he asked Pike to leave Indian Territory with his regiments. Those units were raised only to defend Indian Territory.

MAH: You mentioned the Battle of Wilson's Creek. There are various accounts of "sightings" of Indian troops at that earlier battle outside Indian Territory. Do you know of any Indian units present there?

CDK: Based on reliable research by Dr. William Piston, I would have to conclude that there were no organized Indian regiments at Wilson's Creek.

MAH: Exactly how did the two Cherokee regiments participate in the Battle of Pea Ridge?

CDK: They were part of a combined attack of Cherokee and Texas troops on Elbert's Missouri Battery in the opening phases in the Leetown sector of the battle. [Note: the Confederate Army of the West was divided by Pea Ridge on the first day of the battle, with one column directed towards the hamlet of Leetown and the other towards Elkhorn Tavern.] I would add that I don't believe stories that the Cherokees were the first to reach the battery's guns. Pike admitted that half of his troops were dismounted and that they were at the tail end of the western Confederate column. It's not credible that they could have quickly forced their way through the woods at the west end of Pea Ridge and captured the cannon before Ben McCulloch's mounted regiments reached them.

However, they did participate in fighting around the battery, and they did inflict and receive casualties.

MAH: Many accounts charge that the Cherokee regiments became hopelessly disorganized after the capture of Elbert's Battery. Do you believe this?

CDK: Absolutely. Pike says that the troops of his command [the Cherokees plus Otis Welch's Texas cavalry squadron) soon refused to take orders from anyone, even Pike himself. I should add that the Texas cavalry in the vicinity were equally uncontrollable. Both the Cherokees and the cavalry were apparently riding around in every fashion, firing their weapons in the air and yelling. The excitement of capturing the guns led to a state of disorganization. In contrast, the Arkansas and Louisiana infantry a bit further east maintained their formations.

MAH: What are your conclusions about the infamous scalpings in the area where Pike's troops were involved? I suppose this issue is unavoidable when discussing the Indian troops at Pea Ridge.

CDK: A historian wouldn't want to avoid it. I am personally convinced that some scalpings did take place and that the Cherokee were to blame. Recently Albert Pike's biographer, Walter Brown [see the recommended reading list below], uncovered evidence on the scalpings that seems incontrovertible. Among the documents is an affidavit signed by Pike stating that he saw one of his soldiers shoot and kill a wounded Federal after he fell into the Cherokees' hands. A surgeon who claimed to have tended the wounded of both sides also personally saw at least one dead Federal soldier scalped. In addition, Pike firmly admitted that scalping occurred in correspondence with Samuel Curtis [commander of the Union Army of the Southwest], while countering exaggerations of its extent.

MAH: You recently came across additional information regarding these scalpings at Pea Ridge. Could you share that with our readers?

CDK: Sure. First, any of your readers doing genealogical research will be interested in visiting this web site: www.nacr.net I highly recommend it. This is the Native American Cemetery Readers Genealogy Database Web Site. The site director was kind enough to provide me just last week with the names of the Union Soldiers from the 3rd Iowa Cavalry who were scalped at Pea Ridge. [These names, published here for the first time, are as follows: Private David Carroll, Company B; Private Carroll Foster, Company A (reported scalped but not found); Private Casper Freich, Company B (reported scalped but not found); Private Elisha Ham, Company A; Sgt. Ralph Millard, Company C; Private Spence Miner, Company D].

MAH: This is fascinating information. . . .

CDK: It is wonderful to finally be able to associate some names with the scaplings. I am a bit baffled, though, regarding two soldiers (Foster and Freich). How they can be reported scalped but not found is a bit of a mystery. I checked all these names against the *Roster and Record of Iowa Soldiers in the War of the Rebellion*. Each of these men are listed as being killed at Pea Ridge March 7, 1862. Carroll, Ham, Millard, and Miner are all confirmed to be buried in Fayetteville National Cemetery.

MAH: The prospect has been raised, by historian Edwin C. Bearss among others, that Texas troops might also have participated in scalping at Pea Ridge. In fact, Texans might have had a more recent history of scalping than did the Cherokee, as Texas supposedly paid a bounty for Comanche Indian scalps.

CDK: I have heard that theory, and it's interesting and worthy of further research. However, right now the documentary evidence is that the scalpings were committed by Cherokees.

I'd like to say that the questions of who did the scalpings and of how many men were scalped are interesting but that the scalpings were insignificant. The highest credible number of scalpings I can find is only eight—that's in the *Official Records*. Indians—and white men—had been killing and scalping one another for hundreds of years prior to the Battle of Pea Ridge. You have to expect that the atrocities of war will be different when fighting people from a different culture. Was the killing and mangling of thousands of men at Pea Ridge by other means less terrible? Also, if I were a Native American, I'd be much more concerned and alarmed about atrocities committed by white troops at Sand Creek, the Washita River, and Wounded Knee. We must also acknowledge the murder of black Union soldiers at Poison Springs, Arkansas, and at Jenkins' Ferry, Arkansas, during the Camden Expedition in 1864, and black troops taking their revenge by murdering wounded or captured white Confederates. Combat atrocities are not limited to one race alone.

MAH: Speaking of the Sand Creek Massacre, some combatants at Pea Ridge lost relatives in that event, did they not?

CDK: Yes, there were Cheyenne as well as Cherokees at Pea Ridge. George and Charley Bent were the sons of Santa Fe Trail trader William Bent and his Southern Cheyenne [Tsistsistas] wife, Owl Woman. The boys were in St. Louis in 1861 when Nathaniel Lyon, the commander of the United States arsenal there, captured an encampment of Missouri militia and a riot ensued. The Bents then joined the Missouri State Guard, which fought alongside Confederate troops at Pea Ridge. The Bents followed the MSG into regular Confederate service, but by 1864 they were back with their mother's people in Colorado. George was serving as an emissary of Chief Black Kettle at the time that Black Kettle's band was decimated at Sand Creek. [See the article on John M. Chivington in this issue for more information on Sand Creek.]

MAH: How assimilated into white customs were the Indian troops at Pea Ridge? A well-known Currier and Ives lithograph and the popular imagination paint the Indian troops as very exotic in appearance. However, Texas commissioners to the "Five Civilized Tribes" claimed that the members were "rapidly becoming a nation of whites."

CDK: The Cherokees in particular were very assimilated. They owned slaves, and in this and other ways were more attuned to the Southern white way of life than to the Northern way of life. Period photos show then wearing white-style American clothing. We don't know how the Cherokee were clothed at Pea Ridge in particular. The oral traditions are in conflict. Some accounts indicate that for battle they wore more traditional clothing: ribbon shirts, turbans, and the like. However, equally reliable traditions state that they didn't differ in appearance from Anglos from east Texas. We just don't know for sure.

MAH: What became of the Indian regiments at Pea Ridge after the battle?

CDK: Drew's would become the only Civil War regiment I can think of that deserted as a mass to the enemy. This shows how weak the tribal allegiance was to the Confederacy cause. Watie's Second Cherokee Regiment [which was redesignated as the First after Drew's defection] continued to do good service for the Confederacy in Indian Territory. Watie was even promoted to the rank of brigadier general, becoming the highest ranking Native American in the war. He was the last Confederate general officer to surrender his command, though that may have been largely because his was among the farthest west and was a least a month late getting word of other surrenders. Various Cherokee units resisted Federal movements into what is now northeastern Oklahoma. They hampered Federal operations routed though Indian Territory and scored some minor victories, like the one at Second Cabin Creek [September 19, 1864; see the article in this issue]. The Cherokee would later pay the price for this resistance in land seizures following the war, despite the fact that a majority of the tribe remained neutral or eventually committed to the Union cause. As author Laurence Hauptmann has pointed out, if anybody clearly lost the war it was the Indians.

MAH: How similar were the veteran Confederate Indians to other Trans-Mississippi theater veterans?

CDK: My sense is that they were very similar. The farther west you went the less and less it was the type of gentleman's war supposedly fought east of the Appalachian Mountains. You don't have a George Custer doffing his hat to the enemy like you do in one story from the Eastern Theater. In the Trans-Mississippi you have people like Bloody Bill Anderson riding around with Union soldiers' scalps on his saddle. The Trans-Mississippi West was the professional soldiers' worst nightmare because here there was a war of amateurs. I get the impression that for many soldiers this far west, Indian or white, there was less allegiance to a side than there was a concern for what they could get out of the situation.

MAH: You're familiar with the postwar soldiers of the Western frontier army following the war. How similar would they have been to the soldiers in the West during the war?

CDK: You have to remember that during the Civil War there was a distinction between troops early in the war and later in the war. Early on, troops were almost all volunteers, and their participation was based largely on their convictions. Later, many men were draftees, forced into service. The postwar frontier Regulars enlisted for service, but in many ways their attitudes and experiences were more like that those of the Civil War draftees. They often joined the postwar army because of problems or lack of opportunities back east rather than because of any principles. They seldom had the lust for glory or fame that had motivated the Civil War volunteers of 1861.

Some of the frontier volunteers had served in the Civil War and had already lost any romantic view of military life. They had seen men die of illnesses like diarrhea, measles, and various camp maladies, seen multiple amputations, slept in freezing mud. The life of a postwar frontier regular was no more romantic--it was often dull and monotonous. Recruits handled a shovel a lot more than they did a Springfield rifle. There were frequent problems with alcohol due to the Regulars' isolation and their being stuck in winter quarters with nothing but other men for company.

MAH: Changing the subject to leaders, Albert Pike was a pivotal figure in the West early in the war. His abilities and his negative opinion of Confederate treatment of the Indian tribes remains controversial. What is your own opinion of the man?

CDK: Pike certainly was a central figure in the West in the early days of the War, having served as the Confederate Indian commissioner before the fighting broke out. He was the man who successfully negotiated the major treaties with the tribes. As a diplomat and a statesmen, Pike was vital. As a military leader, he left much to be desired. I don't think that he was the military idiot that some historians have made him out to be. I think that he was simply promoted beyond his abilities, as often happens. He did not have the right education to be a high-ranking officer. He was unskilled in strategy and was promoted because of his statesmanship.

MAH: In earlier conversations, you've drawn parallels between George Custer at Little Bighorn, where you used to work, and Earl Van Dorn at Pea Ridge, where you work now. Could you touch on that?

Brigadier General Albert Pike

National Archives

CDK: In both battles, the commanders allowed a separation of forces, Custer by the Little Bighorn River, Van Dorn by Pea Ridge. They could not reassemble their forces in time and lost control of their battles. Custer could have learned something from Van Dorn's defeat—not that he would have. Both men were both very dashing and flamboyant, even by the standards of their time. Of course, unlike Custer, Van Dorn carried this flamboyance into his relations with the ladies, which eventually got him killed by an irate husband rather than in battle. Both men were also very aggressive officers, which I frankly admire. There were times when hesitation, as in the case of [Union Army of the Potomac commander] George McClellan, was not wise.

MAH: Doug, it must be a very different experience working at Pea Ridge rather than at Little Bighorn. For one thing, only a fraction of the Little Bighorn

Battlefield is federally protected, whereas almost all of Pea Ridge is protected. For another, Pea Ridge has an extensive trail system, whereas foot access at Little Bighorn was limited to one trail until this last summer. Do you find that land protection and trail access is important in interpreting and understanding a battlefield? [The administration of Little Bighorn Battlefield decided in the late 1980s to prohibit foot traffic except upon a previously paved trail at the detached Reno-Benteen sector of the battlefield. This past summer, Superintendent Neil Mangum, after further environmental assessment, opened two additional seasonal trails. For more information on the trails and on the land preservation campaign at Little Bighorn, see the news section of this issue.]

CDK: The advantage to having public foot access to a battlefield is a "no brainer"—it doesn't take any deep thought to understand how meaningful it or is why it's important. Parks belong to the public. If we don't allow trail access, there's no sense having a park. I would agree that protecting the resources in a park from injury has to come before any other priority. But if we can figure out how to put a space shuttle into orbit, we can figure out how to construct trails that provide reasonable access within a park with minimal impact.

Concerning preservation, even a park like Pea Ridge has problems. I'd say that about 80 percent of the battlefield would still be recognizable to the soldiers who fought here, but certainly not 100 percent. Arkansas Highway 72 forms our southwest boundary and cuts through the Leetown sector. U.S. Highway 62 also cuts though the park, creating a serious problem in the viewshed. To the great credit of [former Chief Historian for the National Park Service] Ed Bearss and the people of Arkansas, all of the actual combat area has been protected in the park. But no one foresaw what would happen to the setting with the rapid growth of northwest Arkansas. This would explain why there are groups like the Custer Battlefield Preservation Committee trying to protect the Little Bighorn Battlefield while they still can. When I was at Little Bighorn, I used to watch the moon rise to the southeast over the Wolf Mountains. I realized how fortunate I was to be able to see the land as the Sioux and Cheyenne must have seen it or even as their ancestors had when the land was newly emerged from ancient seas. I would like to see that unchanged.

MAH: Doug, this has been an enlightening conversation. Thank you for your time.

CDK: You're welcome. I enjoyed speaking with you.

For more information on Indian participation in the Battle of Pea Ridge, Arkansas, *JIW* recommends Walter Lee Brown, *A Life of Albert Pike* (Fayetteville: University of Arkansas Press, 1997); Michael A. Hughes, "A Forgotten Battle in a Region Ignored: Pea Ridge," *Blue & Gray Magazine*, 5, no. 3 (January 1988); and William Shea and Earl Hess, *Pea Ridge: Civil War Campaign in the West* (Chapel Hill: University of North Carolina Press, 1992).

WISCONSIN'S 1832 BLACK HAWK WAR TRAIL

Dave Gjeston

T he Black Hawk War was the last armed conflict between Indians and Euro-American settlers in the Old Northwest Territory (now much of the U.S. Midwest). The conflict resulted from misunderstandings and mistakes that ultimately destroyed a remarkable Indian leader and stained the United States' victory with shame and embarrassment. Historical markers tracing Black Hawk's path through Wisconsin are now in place, enabling visitors to travel the route and learn of the events.

On April 5, 1832, Black Hawk [Makataimeshekiakiak] led a group of about 1,000 Sac, Fox [*Mesquakie*], and Kickapoo men, women, and children west from Iowa into Illinois. He and his followers had repudiated a treaty depriving them of their traditional homeland east of the Mississippi River. They intended to reoccupy Black Hawk's former main village, Saukenuk [now Rock Island], with the expectation that area tribes and the British would come to his aid and throw the Americans out of the territory. [For the most recent analysis of these events, see Patrick J. Jung, "The Black Hawk War Reconsidered," *Journal of the Indian Wars,* Vol. 1, No. 2, pp. 31-69.] Black Hawk soon learned that help was not in the offering and that American soldiers were on their way from St. Louis to force his return to Iowa.

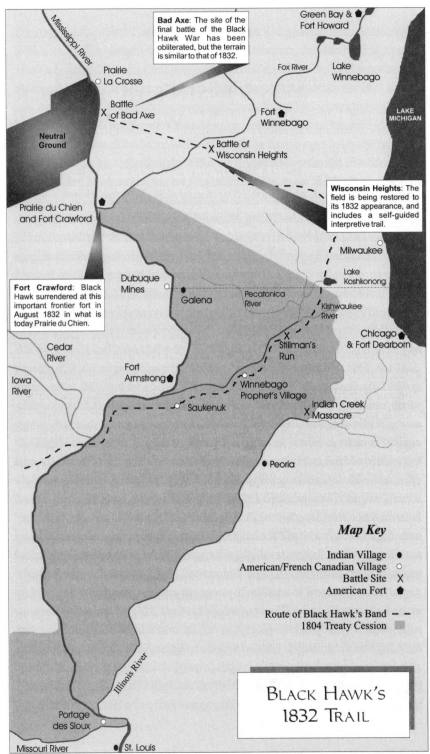

Bad Axe: The site of the final battle of the Black Hawk War has been obliterated, but the terrain is similar to that of 1832.

Wisconsin Heights: The field is being restored to its 1832 appearance, and includes a self-guided interpretive trail.

Fort Crawford: Black Hawk surrendered at this important frontier fort in August 1832 in what is today Prairie du Chien.

Mississippi River

Green Bay & Fort Howard

Prairie La Crosse

Fox River

Lake Winnebago

LAKE MICHIGAN

Battle of Bad Axe

Fort Winnebago

Neutral Ground

Battle of Wisconsin Heights

Prairie du Chien and Fort Crawford

Milwaukee

Lake Koshkonong

Dubuque Mines

Galena

Pecatonica River

Kishwaukee River

Chicago & Fort Dearborn

Cedar River

Stillman's Run

Iowa River

Fort Armstrong

Winnebago Prophet's Village

Indian Creek Massacre

Saukenuk

Peoria

Map Key

Indian Village ●
American/French Canadian Village ○
Battle Site X
American Fort ⬟

Route of Black Hawk's Band — —
1804 Treaty Cession ▪

BLACK HAWK'S 1832 TRAIL

Illinois River

Portage des Sioux

Missouri River   St. Louis

Theodore P. Savas

Over the next two months, the U.S. military, under the leadership of Gen. Henry Atkinson, futilely searched for Black Hawk's followers throughout northern Illinois. Augmented by militia called up by Illinois Gov. John Reynolds, the search eventually led northeasterly up the Rock River towards the great wilderness of the Wisconsin portion of Michigan Territory. On May 14 at Old Man's Creek, Illinois, Black Hawk's pursuers suffered a military disaster known as "Stillman's Run," named after the officer in charge of the Illinois volunteers, Maj. Isaiah Stillman. Black Hawk had been attempting to negotiate his people's safe return to Iowa, but Stillman's men, groggy from drinking whiskey the previous evening, misunderstood the negotiators' intentions. When the disorderly solders pursued the Indian representatives, they ran into an ambush that had been set up by Black Hawk and forty warriors. Although the Indians were outnumbered at least three to one, the surprise was so complete that the soldiers not only ran from the battlefield, but back through their encampment and west to Dixon's Ferry, a distance of thirty miles. Some Illinois militiamen simply quit the war at that point and went home.

When General Atkinson entered the future state of Wisconsin at an abandoned Winnebago camp called Turtle Village (now Beloit, Wisconsin) on July 1, he was confident that his federal troops were finally catching up with Black Hawk's band. Continuing north along the Rock River and led by Winnebago Indian scouts, the U.S. Regulars searched the Lake Koshkonong area, expecting a battle at any moment. Except for a blind Sac elder in another abandoned camp, however, they did not find a trace of the chief's followers.

After scouring the lake area and suffering through the mud and mosquitoes of horrendous swamps and difficult marches, the military ran out of provisions. General Atkinson began constructing a fort at the intersection of the Rock River and White Water Creek/Bark River and sent two regiments off for supplies; one regiment proceeded west to Fort Hamilton, the other north to Fort Winnebago. The northern contingent was led by Gens. James Henry and Milton Alexander and contained the nation's first "mounted rangers," these being Michigan Territory volunteers led by Col. Henry Dodge. On July 18, as Henry and Alexander's regiment prepared for its return trip, one of its Winnebago scouts discovered Black's Hawk's route heading west, and the pursuit was on.

The trail west led to the "area of the Four Lakes" (now Madison, Wisconsin). While passing across the north end of the Third Lake [Lake Monona] late on July 20, the Federal advance spotted Black Hawk's rear guard and halted for the night. The next day, army spies inflicted the first Indian casualty of the campaign by killing one of Black Hawk's men near the Third Lake's west shore. It was later learned that the "warrior" was an elderly Sac mourning at the freshly dug grave of his wife. That same day the soldiers located Black Hawk's abandoned camp near the Fourth Lake [Lake Mendota] as they continued west. With abandoned camp equipment and various trails clearly indicating the direction of flight, the military's pursuit became so frenzied that some forty horses gave out over the next twenty miles.

By the afternoon of July 21, Black Hawk arrived at a Wisconsin River crossing familiar to the Sauk nation from its occupation of the vicinity [that of modern Sauk City] in the early 1700s. High water forced the Indians to take time to make rafts and primitive canoes to reach the north side. Scouts reported that U.S. troops were rapidly approaching, so Black Hawk selected about fifty warriors to return with him to a nearby bluff (Wisconsin Heights) to slow the soldiers' advance and gain time for his followers to cross the river. About twenty warriors under Principal Chief Neopope were positioned east of Black Hawk's men as a rear guard and screening force.

Henry's advance was led by members of the Spy Battalion (i.e., reconnaissance battalion), under Maj. William L. D. Ewing. Ewing's men charged across tall prairie grass in a steady rain but were twice halted when Neopope's party attacked their front and left flank. The soldiers managed to spot what seemed to be the main Indian position farther west. Colonel Dodge, meanwhile, had been pushing his territorial volunteers hard, and they arrived ahead of the U.S. Regulars. Dodge and Ewing combined forces and advanced until they found Black Hawk's main force occupying high ground on their left. The Wisconsin River crossing was now only a mile away. Dodge and Ewing's scouts scurried out of the way as Black Hawk's men made a frontal attack from the heights. Repulsed by Dodge's troops, the Indians tried his left flank and again met strong resistance. When Henry and the Regulars arrived, bringing the entire U.S. force to over 700 men, Black Hawk settled into a holding action.

Henry's troops could see the Indian leader on a nearby hill. He was mounted on a white horse and, with his loud distinct voice, could even be heard by the soldiers as he shouted out encouragement and commands to his warriors. The troops kept up a steady fire from .69 and .75 caliber muskets for almost an hour before Dodge and other officers recommended a bayonet charge to General Henry. Henry approved immediately and ordered the advance. The heavily outnumbered Indians were driven from the high ground but escaped into the nearby marshland of the Wisconsin River bottoms, where the high grass concealed them. The difficulty of pursuit and the coming of nightfall brought the Battle of Wisconsin Heights to a close.

Henry recalled his troops and returned to the battlefield. His concern now was setting up camp, taking care of his eight wounded, and preparing to bury his only fatality, Pvt. Thomas Jefferson Short. For some reason, all of the Indian guides, Winnebago, Menominee, and Potawatomi, were sent to Fort Winnebago. At 3:00 a.m. the next morning, a loud voice was heard shouting in Winnebago. Indecipherable without the scouts, the words were taken to be attack commands. Henry assembled his men and shouted words of encouragement to them as they prepared for an assault. The voice was heard for almost another hour, but nothing happened. A scouting party searched the area and found only fresh horse tracks, signs that someone had climbed a tree, and a symbolically buried tomahawk. Black Hawk had just made a second unsuccessful attempt to negotiate a surrender.

Early on the morning of July 22, Henry led his men to the riverbank still expecting another battle. However, the Indians had successfully crossed the river and had vanished. Henry's soldiers returned to the heights of the battlefield for another day of rest before heading southerly to Blue Mounds Fort (today the community of Blue Mounds) to resupply. General Atkinson met Henry at the fort and set out with a force of 1,300 Regulars and militia to return to the Wisconsin River and continue the pursuit. After a delay of three days crossing the river, scouts relocated Black Hawk's trail.

The next several days proved hard traveling as the trail led through torturous thickets and over rugged hills northwesterly towards the Mississippi River. The soldiers received word July 29 that a portion of Black Hawk's followers had been intercepted and killed or captured on the Wisconsin River near its confluence with the Mississippi. Henry's forces finally encountered Black Hawk's rear guard again on August 2, and a skirmish with it drew some of the soldiers north. In the meantime, however, Dodge's mounted militia and Henry's Regular brigade swung south and west to prevent an Indian escape across the Mississippi. In the process, the troops blundered into Black Hawk's main force near the junction of the Mississippi and the Bad Axe River. The resulting battle soon became a slaughter as the greatly outnumbered Indians were overwhelmed. Men, women, and children alike were shot down in the smoke and confusion. Many Indians drowned trying to escape across the river. The gun ship *Warrior* blocked escape by water and added devastating artillery fire to the battle.

After the killing ended, Atkinson learned that Black Hawk was gone. He had recently attempted to surrender a third time, this time to the *Warrior's* captain, Joseph Throckmorton. Suspecting trickery, however, Throckmorton had opened fire on the band on the riverbank. At that, Black Hawk left with three of his followers in an attempt to escape north. Although Black Hawk had started to return on August 2, he had arrived at a bluff overlooking the river just in time to see that he could do nothing to save his people from the slaughter taking place below and then had left.

On August 28, 1832, Black Hawk turned himself over to two Winnebagos to be escorted to Fort Crawford. At that fort he was placed in chains and taken down river to Fort Armstrong. Later he and several companions were taken to Washington, D.C., and after a year's imprisonment in Virginia were paraded up and down the east coast for almost a year to impress upon them the tremendous population of the United States and the futility of further resistance.

Black Hawk returned to Iowa to serve quietly under his rival Keokuk, a new Sac and Fox chief appointed by the U.S. government. Black Hawk died peacefully October 3, 1838. A year earlier, less than five years after his defeat, he was already being feted by former enemies as a hero at a Wisconsin banquet.

What to See

The Black Hawk War Trail offers touring opportunities by car on a route marked with historical monuments which pay tribute to various war events or the war's participants. For information on obtaining a brochure and the booklet *The Battle of Wisconsin Heights & the Black Hawk War of 1832*, contact Department of Natural Resources, 101 S. Webster Street, Box 7921, Madison, WI 53707-7921.

In addition to terrain similar to that of 1832, visitors on the driving tour can see the following historic sites:

1. Fort Atkinson: A full-sized replica of the fort is located on the west side of Fort Atkinson off State Highway 106.

2. Wisconsin Heights: The Department of Natural Resources (DNR) purchased most of the Wisconsin Heights Battleground in 1990 as part of the Lower Wisconsin State Riverway project, though the precise location was not pinpointed until 1995. The battlefield is now being restored to its 1832 condition, when it was in oak savannah vegetation. A self-guided interpretive

trail was completed in the summer of 1998. Prehistoric Indian mounds can also be seen at the site. The Sac and Fox Nation has established a partnership with the DNR to support site restoration efforts. Planning for public education involving the site will also include participation by the other nations represented at the battle, including the Ho-Chunk, Kickapoo, Menominee, and Potawatomi tribes.

3. Pecatonica (Bloody Lake): The battle site is surrounded by country park lands two miles northwest of Woodford. The oxbow lake where the battle was fought is still evident.

4. Fort Blue Mounds: The fort's configuration can still be seen at this archaeological site and monument.

5. Military Trail: State Highway 18 from Blue Mounds west to the Wisconsin River roughly follows the west segment of the trail, which eventually finds its way to Green Bay.

6. Fort Union: Col. Henry Dodge's cabin and lead mining center are located two miles south of Dodgeville off State Highway 23 on County Road Y.

7. Fort Crawford: This important frontier fort in what is today the town of Prairie du Chien is the location of Black Hawk's surrender on August 22, 1832.

8. Bad Axe: This site of final battle of the war is located three miles south of Victory on the Mississippi River. The actual battle site has been obliterated, but the floodplain terrain is similar to what was present in 1832.

Further Reading

Hagan, William T., *Black Hawk's Route Through Wisconsin* (The State Historical Society of Wisconsin, 1949).

Jung, Patrick J., "The Black Hawk War Reconsidered," *Journal of the Indian Wars,* Vol. 1, No. 2 (Savas Publishing, 1999), 31-69.

Tyler, Crawford, *Chasing a Shadow: The Search for Black Hawk* (Banta Press, 1981).

——, *The Battle of Wisconsin Heights* (Banta Press, 1983).

——, *Massacre at Bad Axe* (Banta Press, 1984).

THE INDIAN WARS

Organizational, Battlefield, and Museum News

T his column is reserved for information concerning issues of archaeology and preservation, reenactments and commemorations, organizational and educational events, art exhibits, and tribal events. We welcome information, news clippings, and press releases.

JIW is pleased to announce that Jerry L. Russell, national chairman of the Order of the Indian Wars and a leader in the preservation of Indian wars and Civil War battlefields, will offer an online historic preservation column on the Internet. The new column will be hosted at www.savaspublishing.com.

Fallen Timbers Battlefield, 1794. During the summer and fall of 1999, the United States House of Representatives and Senate passed the Fallen Timbers Battlefield and Fort Miamis National Historical Site Act. [See *JIW* Vol. 1, No. 2 for more information about Fallen Timbers.] The legislation establishes an affiliated, non-federal area of the National Park System outside Maumee and Toledo, Ohio. The new park will include 194 acres of the Fallen Timbers battlefield (the most important in the Indian wars of the early U.S. republic), the non-adjacent memorial, and what has been the Fort Miamis Municipal Park of the city of Maumee. The National Park Service will provide technical support during the development of the sites for visitation.

Revolutionary War and War of 1812. In 1996, the U.S. Congress authorized major funding for the study of the battlefields of the Revolutionary War and the War of 1812. The two studies were to be similar to the massive undertaking done for American Civil War battlefields. After Congress failed to appropriate financing, the National Park Service found it necessary to redirect part of its battlefield preservation grant funds to begin the projects. During 2000, the park service's American Battlefield Protection Program (ABPP) will begin to inventory and survey the principal military sites of the two conflicts.

Several important Indian wars battlefields associated with the Revolution likely to be surveyed include Newtown in New York, Long Island Flat in Tennessee, and Point Pleasant in West Virginia. During the War of 1812 study, several battlefields of the Creek War and sites associated with the Shawnee leader Tecumseh should be surveyed. ABPP *Battlefield Update* newsletters may be obtained from National Park Service, Heritage Preservation Services, American Battlefield Protection Program, 1849 C Street, NW (NC330), Washington, D.C. 20240. *Battlefield Update* can also be found on the Internet at www2.cr.nps.gov/abpp/.

Sand Creek Massacre Site, 1864. The location of the Sand Creek Massacre has long been, like the event itself, the subject of controversy. In the fall of 1864, Sand Creek, in eastern Colorado, was the refuge of Black Kettle's band of Southern Cheyenne and some Arapahos. Black Kettle believed that his people were protected by an amnesty with the governor of Colorado, the assurance of officers at Fort Lyon, and the flying of an American flag. However, in the predawn hours of November 29, 1864, the encampment was attacked by Colorado volunteer troops led by Col. John M. Chivington. [See Patrick Bowmaster's biographical column on Chivington in this issue.] Chivington's men killed an estimated 150 to 200 Indians, perhaps two-thirds of whom were women and children.

By the 1970s, there were serious doubts that the location in modern Kiowa County commemorating the attack was accurate. Metal detector hobbyists had repeatedly failed to find any evidence of an engagement around the site of the 1950 monument. In addition, members of the Sand Creek Descendent Association said that Cheyenne tradition placed the camp elsewhere. The Colorado Historical Society began a study to locate the site, but was unsuccessful. In 1998, Senator Ben Nighthorse Campbell [Republican, Colorado] introduced legislation directing the National Park Service (NPS) to locate the site. The legislation was signed into law on October 6, 1998.

As the legislation directed, the NPS consulted on the project with the Northern Cheyenne, Northern Arapaho, and the Southern Cheyenne and Arapaho Tribes of Oklahoma, as well as with the State of Colorado. Work began soon after the legislation passed, and NPS historians and archaeologists renewed efforts to document the whereabouts of the massacre site. Tribal oral histories, historical archival research, aerial photography, geomorphic studies, photographic interpretation, and interviews with local residents contributed to the body of data archaeologists needed to begin field investigations in late May of 1999.

With financial assistance from the American Battlefield Protection Program, the Intermountain Region of the NPS finally concluded a successful search for the elusive site late during the summer of 1999. NPS archaeologist Doug Scott of the Midwest Archaeological Center in Lincoln, Nebraska, led an interagency team consisting of volunteer professionals from the NPS, the Bureau of Land Management, the U.S. Forest Service, and the Oklahoma Historical Society. Members of the Southern Cheyenne, Northern Cheyenne, Southern Arapaho, and Northern Arapaho tribes, and local landowners were also active in the archaeological fieldwork. The field team spent two weeks working its way upstream along Sand Creek, focusing on an area that historical research and Cheyenne oral history indicated was the most likely candidate for the site of Black Kettle's village.

At an undisclosed point over a mile from the commemorated site, the archaeologists began to uncover over 300 period artifacts. These included shell fragments from artillery of the type known to have bombarded the camp (12-pounder cannonballs), other ammunition, a cast iron kettle, cooking pot fragments, tin cups and plates, utensils, iron arrowheads, and personal ornaments. According to Scott, "The artifacts are mid-19th century in date and are consistent with the types of materials found archaeologically in other Native American villages of the same time period. There is little doubt that we have found the camp attacked by the Colorado Volunteer Cavalry." He also noted that the low percentage of projectiles fired by Indians versus non-Indians substantiates the consensus that the engagement was a massacre.

The archaeological fieldwork capped the first phase of this project, which was to find the Sand Creek Massacre site; the NPS is completing a site location report. The second phase of the project, preparing a Special Resource Study outlining management alternatives for the site, began in October. *JIW* will continue to carry updated developments on this important and ongoing research.

(Sources: American Battlefield Protection Program; *Archaeology*, 52, no. 6 (November/December 1999)

One of the more unusual sites on the World Wide Web posts the inventory notices given in accordance with provisions of the Native American Graves Protection and Repatriation Act (NAGPRA). As the act's title suggests, this fairly recent statue provides U.S. protection for Indian human remains. In addition, the act obligates museums and federal agencies to determine the cultural affiliation of remains and associated funerary objects under their control and to publish the results of their inventories. The assessments are often made in consultation with modern tribal governments. The "Notices of Inventory Completion" may be found on the World Wide Web at www.cast.uark.edu/other/nagpra/nic.html, one of the pages of the National Archeological Database.

Some of the inventoried remains were collected from Indian wars battlefields by soldiers, relic hunters, and archaeologists. For example, Notice 215 of July 1998, deals with a scalp lock taken from the Sand Creek Massacre site [1864], probably by Maj. Jacob Downing, and eventually donated to the Colorado Historical Society. The scalp lock may substantiate reports of mutilations of dead Cheyenne and Arapaho by Colorado volunteers at Sand Creek. Notice 241 of October 1998, describes bone fragments excavated by the Nebraska State Historical Society from what appears to be a battlefield grave dug at the site of the final engagement between the U.S. Army and Dull Knife's band of Cheyennes during Dull Knife's escape from Fort Robinson, Nebraska [1879]. Both state historical societies consulted with the Cheyenne-Arapaho Tribes of Oklahoma and the Northern Cheyenne Tribe of the Northern Cheyenne Reservation.

Fort Phil Kearney, Bozeman Trail War, 1866-68. During 1999, the Fort Phil Kearney/Bozeman Trail Association made progress in raising the $38,000 needed to match a Wyoming Department of Transportation grant for archaeological work and reconstruction at the site of Fort Phil Kearney. The fort was one of the two "hot points" of the 1866-68 conflict known as the "Bozeman Trail War," "First Sioux War," or "Red Cloud's War." During the year the LTA archaeological firm did site mapping, remote sensing, and excavation at the site, revealing portions of the stockade footing in the process. The report of the findings will be delivered in mid-2000. Donations, membership fees ($15 per year), and inquiries may be sent to Robert McBride, P.O. Box 82834, or to Mary Ellen McWilliams, 10004 Big Goose Road, Sheridan, WY 82801.

The Frontier Heritage Alliance is an fairly recent organization hoping to bring together a variety of organizations, agencies, tribes, and institutions working for the preservation, interpretation, and development of their "shared heritage on the Northern Plains." The alliance has already helped bring about a number of achievements of great interest to students of the Indian wars. These include the honoring of the Cheyenne with markers at Little Bighorn Battlefield, the upgrading of Chief Plenty Coups' home in Montana to the status of a National Historic Landmark, and the June 21st ground breaking for the five million dollar National Historic Trails Center at Casper, Wyoming. The alliance also helped secure a $21,600 grant from the American Battlefield Protection Program for a study and action plan for six battlefields involved in General George Crook's 1876 campaign on the Northern Plains. The grant project will be supervised by retired NPS employee and scholar John D. McDermott. The alliance will also play a role in Bozeman Trail Days in June (see below) and in the 32nd Annual Dakota Conference. Contact Frontier Heritage Alliance, 1004 Big Goose Road, Sheridan, WY 82801 or jmcwill@wavecom.net (e-mail is preferred). The Frontier Heritage Alliance's web site may be found at www.wavecom.net/frontieralliance/index.html.

Washita Battlefield, 1868. In the fall of 1999, the National Park Service released for public comment four draft alternatives for the development of the new Washita Battlefield National Historic Site. [For much more information on the battle at this site, see *JIW*, Vol. 1, No. 1.] The current development of the battlefield is largely limited to an overlook and a temporary trail without signboards. Alternative A is the "Existing Conditions/No Action" option. Alternative B, the "Window into the Past" option, proposes a visitor center in a facility one mile off the site, a facility to be shared with Black Kettle National Grassland (National Forest Service). Alternative B would provide fairly limited on-site interpretation. Alternative C, the "Integrated Visitor Experience" option, would establish an on-site visitor center and more interpretation than Alternative B. Alternative D, the "Dispersed Visitor Experience" option, calls for maximal on-site interpretation, including a trails system, but proposes that the visitor center again be a mile off the site and in a shared facility. Alternatives B, C, and D all would provide areas for the demonstration and sale of Native American crafts.

The concept of placing the visitor center a mile from the current overlook (alternatives B and D) has much to recommend it. Placing a visitor center near the heart of a battlefield, as in the case of Gettysburg National Battlefield, permanently diminishes the integrity of the site it is intended to commemorate. In addition, an off-site visitor center could be placed on ground offering a panoramic view of the environs of the battlefield, including the place where Maj. Joel Elliott's detachment was annihilated. During 2000, the park service will prepare a draft management plan and an environmental impact statement. To obtain further information on the battlefield's development, write Superintendent, Washita Battlefield National Historic Site, P.O. Box 890, Cheyenne, OK 73628.

The fall conference of the Order of the Indian Wars produced an interesting postscript to an article published in the premiere edition of *JIW*. In "Captain Albert Barnitz and the Battle of the Washita," which appeared in Vol. 1, No. 2, S. Matthew Despain drew upon unpublished documents by Barnitz to revise previous interpretations of the path and role of the Seventh Cavalry's G Company in the 1868 battle. Despain also related how Captain Barnitz had been seriously wounded and sought shelter in a ring of boulders. Barnitz survived, but the effects of his wound forced his retirement from the army within two years. Despain mentioned in conversations with *JIW's* editor Michael Hughes that years ago he saw what he might be the boulders to which Barnitz referred.

On September 19, 1999, members of the Order of the Indian Wars were engaged in a tour of Washita Battlefield National Historic Site. The walking portion utilized the first visitor route opened at the new park, a temporary trail mowed for the 1999 visitor season. The trail passed an embankment thought to

The possible location of Capt. Albert Barnitz's "ring of stone," at the Washita Battlefield National Historic Site. *Courtesy of Michael Hughes*

be the site of the slaughter of the Indian village's ponies, then ascended the bank near a gypsum ledge that is the only outcropping of large stones on the battlefield. The editor was discussing the Barnitz article with novelist Terry Johnston when he noticed five stones which had tumbled from the ledge to form a ring of boulders [see photograph]. The stone circle, very likely the one described by Barnitz, should be easily discernible to future visitors if the current trail route remains in use.

Little Bighorn Battlefield, 1876. The official groundbreaking ceremony for the monument to the Indian participants in the Battle of the Little Bighorn was held on Veterans Day, November 11, 1999. Caleb Shields, former tribal chairman of the Assiniboine and Sioux Tribes, Fort Peck Indian Reservation, opened the ceremonies by blowing an eagle whistle to the four directions.

Following this, Karen Wade, Intermountain Regional Director for the National Park Service remarked that "this hallowed ground must speak for itself and remind us of our mission and our responsibility to future generations." Other participants in the ceremonies included a voluntary honor guard from Fort Hood, Texas, in period-style costume, Northern Cheyenne and Yankton Sioux drum groups, and the Morning Star Chapter of the Northern Cheyenne Vietnam Era Veterans.

After a national design competition and considerable debate over location, a site was chosen for the monument in 1997 that is approximately seventy-five yards northeast of the U.S. Cavalry Monument on Monument Hill ("Last Stand Hill"). Two million dollars in public donations will be required to complete the Indian Memorial, and only $25,000 had been received as of the last report to *JIW*. For more information or to make a contribution, contact National Park Foundation, Indian Memorial Fund, 1101 17th Street, NW, Suite 1102, Washington, D.C. 20250. Checks can also be sent in care of Little Bighorn National Monument, P.O. Box 39, Crow Agency, MT 59022.

Efforts to preserve key portions of Little Bighorn Battlefield are at a critical stage. Only 760 acres of the battlefield are protected by the National Park Service. The Custer Battlefield Preservation Committee (CBPC) has taken the leading role in preserving the hundreds of acres of battlefield outside of current park boundaries. To date, the group has acquired 2,200 acres, on which $309,450 is still owed. In 1999, the CBPC was offered the opportunity to purchase several more important tracts of land. These include the site of the opening phase of the battle (Marcus Reno's initial positions), the site of Sitting Bull's Oglala Lakota village, and the route used by many Indian participants to meet and turn back Custer's column. The committee still requires a total of $2,800,000 to purchase the key 1,000 acres involved. More recently, Medicine Tail Coulee, an important feature on the route to George Custer's final position, was also offered to the CBPC for sale. There is no realistic prospect of federal funding for the land at this time, meaning private and corporate donors must come forward to protect the land, much of which is vulnerable to development. To send donations, contact CBPC, P.O. Box 7, Hardin, MT 59034. For more information, write the address above, e-mail custertours@juno.com, or call (406) 665-1876.

During 1999, the Custer Battlefield Historical and Museum Association continued playing a very active role in preservation issues concerning the Little Bighorn and in promoting scholarship on George Custer and the "Great Sioux

War." During 1999, the group also donated $5,000 to the Custer Battlefield Preservation Committee; $2,000 to the battlefield park; $1,000 to the Little Bighorn Indian Memorial fund; and $8,000 to the Fort Abraham Lincoln Foundation. Members of the organization receive the quarterly publication "The Battlefield Dispatch" and a 15 percent discount on mail order books from an extensive list of books for sale. Membership is only $12.50 per year for a regular membership, $20.00 per year for a Canadian or overseas membership, and $40.00 per year for a sustaining membership. Contact CBHMA, P. O. Box 902, Hardin, MT 59034-0902, phone (406) 665-2060.

[Editor's note: "Custer Battlefield" is the former name of the current Little Bighorn National Battlefield, and the Custer Battlefield Historical and Museum Association continues to use that name. Another organization, the Little Big Horn Associates, prefers to spell the name of the battlefield "Little Big Horn," while the National Park Service and the U.S. Geological Survey use the spelling "Little Bighorn."]

Throughout 1999, Neil Mangum continued to distinguish himself as one of the most effective superintendents in the history of Little Bighorn National Monument. In the process he displayed considerable skills in diplomacy, balancing the demands of Custer "buffs," Indian advocacy groups, and environmentalists. In the late 1980s, all foot traffic in the park, with the exception of one paved trail in the Reno-Benteen battle sector, was restricted out of concern over soil and vegetation damage. After completion of a new environmental study, Mangum opened two seasonal trails in the Custer battle sector. Deep Ravine Trail follows the route of an ill-fated escape attempt by Custer's collapsing command. Keogh/Crazy Horse Trail proceeds to ground where warriors inspired by Crazy Horse overwhelmed Custer's left battalion under Miles Keogh near "Calhoun Hill." There is a good deal of public support for making the two trails permanent. Mangum also oversaw a diverse interpretive program in 1999 that included regular presentations on weapons and tactics, on the topic "Little Bighorn and the American Imagination," and on life in Indian encampments and in the Seventh Cavalry.

Though there are several excellent study and preservation groups concerned with the Little Bighorn Battlefield, perhaps the meatiest source of information on the battlefield park is a privately produced periodical called *Custer/Little Bighorn Battlefield Advocate*. The quarterly, produced by Wayne M. Sarf, is a blend of news clippings, updates on meetings and interpretive

Novelist Terry Johnston at McClellan Creek Battlefield (1874),
Texas Panhandle. Order of the Indian Wars tour, 1999.

Courtesy of Michael Hughes

events, and very spirited editorials. Subscriptions are $15.00 for U.S. subscriptions, $20.00 for non-U.S. subscriptions.

The Order of the Indian Wars commemorated the 125th anniversary of the Red River War at its September annual assembly. Western Historical Organization director Paul Hutton spoke on Phil Sheridan and the war, and Brett Cruse of the Texas Historical Commission came in directly from his ongoing archaeological investigations of Red River War battlefields to report on his progress. Cruse revealed that the commission had just pinpointed the location of the "Lyman's Wagon Train" fight and discovered the true location of the previously mislocated Miles Fight near Red River. [Cruse has agreed to be interviewed by *JIW* on his finds for a forthcoming issue.] Neil Mangum, superintendent of Little Bighorn National Battlefield, was this year's tour leader. In addition to taking the group to Second Adobe Walls and Palo Duro Canyon, Mangum secured permission for the group to tour the publicly inaccessible battlefields at First Adobe Walls (1864) and McClellan Creek. For information on the organization and on future assemblies, contact Jerry L. Russell, Order of the Indian Wars, P. O. Box 7401, Little Rock, AR 72217 (web site: www.lbha.org/oiw.html).

This year's thirty-ninth annual conference of the Western Historical Association, held in September in Portland, Oregon, was one of the most popular in the organization's history. There were no military history sessions, but there were a considerable number of presentations in 1999 on American Indian history. The topics included Indians in film, the economic role of Indian women, the plains environment, Indian self-determination, and Canadian and U.S. treaty rights. The association maintains a web site at www.unm.edu/~wha/. The 2000 meeting will be in San Antonio. The editor and publisher of this journal hope to attend in order to meet more of our readers and potential authors.

Important Indian Wars-Related Meetings in the first half of 2000

February 19, 2000: Third Rocky Mountain Indian Wars Symposium, Arapahoe [sic] Community College, Littleton, Colorado—Dinner and symposium with (at last report) presentations by Brian Pohanka, Jeff Broome, and Kent Bradenberry, and a performance by the Seventh Cavalry Band. The profits will ultimately go to battlefield preservation. For information, contact Kay Oosterhoff, e-mail kayl1876hotmail.com, or phone (303) 420-1933.

April 27-29, 2000: Third Fort Robinson History Conference, Fort Robinson State Park in Crawford, Nebraska—presentations by leading scholars of military and American Indian history (including Dr. Douglas Scott on the archaeological survey of the Sand Creek Massacre site as well as Jerome Greene, Paul Hedren, and John D. McDermott), an authors' book signing session, living history demonstrations, and artillery demonstrations. For information and/or a registration form, contact Nebraska Historical Society, P.O. Box 82554, Lincoln, NE 68501-2554 or call (402) 471-6548.

May 10-14, 2000: CAMP (Council on America's Military Past) Military History Conference, Burlington, Vermont—*JIW* has not yet received information on this conference, but CAMP conferences are usually intensive, with talks on fortifications, regional military history, and tours of historic places. Presumably the Vermont location could produce talks on King Philip's War and other colonial Indian conflicts. For information contact CAMP, 518 W. Why Worry Lane, Phoenix, AZ 85021.

June 16-18, 2000: Bozeman Trail Days (Theme: Digging Up the Past: "The Construction and Reconstruction of Fort Phil Kearney"), Fort Phil Kearney State Historic Site between Buffalo and Sheridan, Wyoming—An archaeology symposium, living history and historic construction demonstrations, and tours of Fort Phil Kearney and its environs. For details, contact Fort Phil Kearney/Bozeman Trail Association, Inc., P.O. Box 5013, Sheridan, WY 82801. The association keeps a regularly updated web site at www.wavecom.net/philKearney/index.htm/.

June 23, 2000: Annual Custer Battlefield and Museum Association Symposium, Hardin Middle School, Hardin, Montana—To submit one-page precis briefs of papers for this symposium, contact Fr. Vincent A. Heir, 7800 Kenrick Road, St. Louis, MO 63229. For more information on this organization, see the information on its 1999 activities elsewhere in "News."

July 20-22, 2000: Little Big Horn Associates, West Point Conference 2000, Holiday Inn, Fishkill, New York—Talks by Judge William Moody on Brig. Gen. Edward S. Godfrey, by Greg Michno on modern army opinion of George Custer, and by Superintendent Neil Mangum on the state of Little Bighorn National Battlefield. There will also be a private tour of the U.S. Military Academy and an optional tour to Elizabeth Custer's homes in Bronxville, New York. The conference officers are Bruce Liddic, 116 Bungalow Terrace, Syracuse, NY 13207 and Jack Manion, 512 California Street, Beverly Hills, FL 34465. The association's web site is at www.lbha.org/newsletter/.

THOMAS ONLINE

Daughters of the Lance: Native American Women Warriors

Rodney G. Thomas

F our times she charged along with the swirl of warriors toward the small group of soldiers and civilians on the island. Each time she came back with more holes in her dress from the near misses of their bullets. But there was no blood upon the garment. She would not be injured or die this day, even though she wished for death. Her husband, Walking Bear, had been killed the year before. Now even her father understood her desire to die, and he had provided her with the horse she rode into battle. By the end of that autumn day in 1868, E'hyoph'sta (Yellow Haired Woman) was firmly set upon the warrior path and on her way to becoming a renowned and respected member of her husband's Cheyenne military society.[1]

E'hyoph'sta was not the first woman to gain legendary status among the Plains tribes. In 1854, a party of five Crow [Absaroka] warriors en route to an Atsina village was met and escorted by Atsina [or "Gros Ventres"] warriors. The two previously hostile tribes had been working towards peace for almost three years.[2] However, when the Atsina warriors recognized the leader of the Crows as one of the most aggressive and renowned of their former enemies, they immediately killed the Crows despite the party's peaceful intent. Normally an intertribal incident involving five deaths might not even have been included in tribal oral tradition. But in this case the Atsina had killed the greatest Crow warrior of their generation. The party's head, Woman Chief, had been a resolute fighter and renowned war leader of the Crow nation for over twenty years.[3]

These women were two of the better known fighters of their times and regions, but they have often been relegated to mere mentions in footnotes and their deeds labeled irrelevant. This is unfortunate, for this obscurity creates a misleading picture of Native American history. In many cases, Indian women played important and sometimes pivotal roles in warfare with both rival Indians and whites. It is not surprising that Indian women's roles in combat have been marginalized, for the role of women in history in general has traditionally been overlooked. Moreover, for a long time there were few women ethnographers, anthropologists, or historians trekking out to the reservations or tribal encampments seeking enlightenment on what other women did or did not do.

One aim of the "Thomas Online" column is to get into the little known and lesser talked about aspects of history, the stuff that makes history both coherent and interesting. This quarter's column highlights some female warriors, interesting and little known women who participated in the "way of the warrior" with all the dash, courage, honor, and fame that were attributed to that way of life. It also suggests further reading and will hopefully encourage further research.

Our first subject, Yellow Haired Woman or E'hyoph'sta' of the Southern Cheyenne [Tsetschestahase] was born about 1826 and died in August 1915, on the Tongue River Reservation in Montana. Unlike most women warriors, she first entered battle intending to die rather than to achieve revenge for a loss. Her husband, Walking Bear, had been killed by an accidental discharge of his own gun in 1867. Her first foray into combat was in the incident described above, an attack on a volunteer company led by Maj. George Forsyth during the 1868 Southern Plains Campaign. Forsyth's command of fifty-one "Plainsmen" was out to find and report the locations of Indian camps so that the inhabitants could be pursued by regular army units and placed on reservations. The fight took place on September 17, 1868, on the Arickaree Fork of the Republican River in Colorado, at a low riverine island later known as "Beecher's Island."

After surrounding the scouting party on the low island, warriors of the Cheyenne Dog Society, or "Dog Soldiers" as they are more commonly known, kept the small force under siege for eight days. Four times E'hyoph'sta, riding a horse given her by her father for the purpose, joined in mounted charges against the scouts. She was not injured in this battle, but her dress was riddled with bullet holes. Although she did not count coup on an enemy in this fight, she was afterwards known and accepted as a warrior.

E'hyoph'sta's next battle was against the Shoshone on Beaver Creek, a stream near the Big Horn Mountains in Montana. Most sources relate that the incident occurred later on 1868, though an account by a warrior named Wooden Leg places it in 1873. Several Plains tribes had concentrated for their great annual autumn buffalo hunts, occasions which were also times for major horse raids. Members of the Cheyenne camp and the nearby Shoshone camps had been out raiding when they made contact and skirmishing broke out. After one particular attack, the Cheyenne chased and trapped a Shoshone war party in a deep ravine. At the end of four days of fighting, all the Shoshone were either dead or captured. One captured Shoshone warrior was about to be questioned by the Dog Soldiers when E'hyoph'sta came up and said she would interrogate him. She raised the Shoshone's arm, stabbed him twice in the armpit, killing him. She then took his scalp. For this act and two other coups counted during the four days' fighting, she was admitted to the Dog Soldier Warrior Society, the society of her husband. No descriptions of just how she made the other two coups have been located.

Woman Chief was one of the most revered Crow warriors who ever lived. Originally a member of the Atsina or "Gros Ventres" tribe, she had been captured by the Crows when only ten years of age. Woman Chief displayed a love of and affinity for warriors' ways soon after her capture and became an expert rider, marksman, and hunter. As such, she became a regular member of Crow raiding and war parties against other Plains peoples.

Woman Chief's original name is lost to history, but the story of how she earned the honorific name "Woman Chief" is still recited by Crow tribal historians. A Crow encounter with five "Blackfoot" (presumably Piegan) raiders produced a standoff. When none of the male Crow warriors with her would answer the Blackfoot challenge to combat, she rode out alone. As the Blackfoot attacked, she killed one with her gun, wounded two others with arrows, and chased the remaining two away. Woman Chief was thereafter accorded the full rights and privileges of a Crow warrior. She was able to recite her deeds at tribal functions and could boast of more warrior acts than most of the men. She even "married" four women to run her lodge.

Woman Chief also gained fame for horse raiding. On one raid against a Blackfoot village, she personally captured over seventy horses and took two scalps. Horse expeditions usually involved one or two "full" warriors, with the remainder of the party made up of any young men anxious to earn the title of warrior under the tutelage and observation of a prominent leader. Not surprisingly, whenever Woman Chief called for such a raid, there was never a lack of participants.

As described earlier, Woman Chief in 1854 set out for a village of the Crow's hereditary enemies, the Atsina or Gros Ventres. She was taking advantage of the truce between the tribes to undergo a pilgrimage in search of members of her family. Tragically, in spite of three years of peace, decades of inter-tribal war conditioned the response of her fellow Atsinas on recognizing her as a famed Crow fighter. She was killed as a result. Woman Chief remains one of the most renowned warriors of her nation, with her memory kept well alive in tribal oral tradition.

The mysterious female warrior known as the "Other Magpie" was in the Crow Scouts contingent working for Brig. Gen. George Crook during the "Centennial Campaign" of 1876. Crook's column was one of three that were to coordinate efforts and force off-reservation Sioux, Cheyenne, and Arapaho to report to tribal agencies. (The other two columns were those of Col. John Gibbon and Brig. Gen. Alfred Terry, the latter containing George A. Custer's ill-fated Seventh Cavalry Regiment.) Crook's movements were screened and scouted by a combination of Crow and Shoshone scouts. On the morning of June 17, 1876, General Crook's 1,300 soldiers and Indian scouts encountered approximately 1,500 Lakota and Cheyenne warriors on the Rosebud River in Montana. The battle involved more U.S. troops and Indians (both as allies and enemies) than any other battle of the Western Indian campaigns and would be one of the most significant in American history.

What is known of Other Magpie's participation at the Rosebud comes from oral history related by a female Crow elder, Pretty Shield, to Frank B. Linderman. Pretty Shield recalled that the Other Magpie had joined the scouts seeking revenge for the death of her brother at the hands of the Lakota ["Sioux"]. The male scouts thought nothing of her going, as women often accompanied such expeditions, though not necessarily to fight. At the Battle of the Rosebud, members of rival Indian nations fought one another with the same vigor as did Indians and white soldiers. It was during one of the Indian versus Indian fights that The Other Magpie and a Crow berdache (see following definition) named Osh-Tisch (Finds-Them-and-Kills-Them) saved the life of a warrior named Bull Snake. ["Berdache" is a term loosely used by non-Indians to refer to Indians with alternative or dual sexual or gender identity]. Bull Snake had been badly wounded by Lakota rifle fire. Osh-Tisch and the Other Magpie rode to his protection, firing at the Lakota even as they turned and charged the two rescuers. The Other Magpie, armed only with a short belt knife and willow coup stick, broke the Lakota charge and counted coup on a Lakota warrior. Osh-Tisch fired at this same Lakota, killing him, and the Other Magpie then took his scalp. Upon her return to her encampment, the Other Magpie took part in the traditional Crow Scalp Dance and danced and celebrated her coup with her male counterparts. Pretty Shield told Linderman that all Crow women knew of the Other Magpie's exploits but that Crow men would not speak of them.

In contrast with many of the Plains peoples, the Cherokee [Tsalagi] were traditionally a matrilineal society, and women have always played key leadership roles in their history. The most prominent of all such women was Nan'yehi or Nancy Ward. Born around 1738 in the Overhill Cherokee portion of the Cherokee Nation, Nan'yehi earned the coveted title of *Ghigua* in battle with the Muskogee or "Creeks" in 1755. This title and accompanying position, the highest that could be earned by and awarded to a female leader, variously translates "Beloved Woman," "Much Honored Woman," and "War Woman."

Nan'yehi married a great warrior, Kingfisher, while still in her teens. The Cherokee and Muskogee territories overlapped in the hills of Georgia, and there was constant warfare between the two nations. During a major battle at a place called Taliwa, Kingfisher was killed. Cherokee and Muskogee women often went into battle, and Nan'yehi had on this occasion. When her husband fell, Nan'yehi picked up his weapon, rallied the Cherokee, and led them to a decisive victory over the Creeks. From that day on, Nan'yehi was recognized as the ghigua.

Nan'yehi now occupied a position with a vote and voice in the General Council, exercised leadership of a Women's Council, and served as a peace negotiator. She was on the one hand a fierce protector of Cherokee rights and on the other a voice arguing for the advantages of adopting some white ways. One of her special privileges was that she held the right to save the life of any prisoner. Using that right, she saved the life of a Mrs. William Bean, who would later help the Cherokees in adopting new practices of weaving, animal husbandry, and land ownership.

As a leading negotiator for the Cherokee during talks in 1785, Nan'yehi signed the Treaty of Hopewell between the United States and the Cherokees. By 1808, however, she was urging the tribe not to sell additional land because she had become convinced that the Cherokee were being systematically pushed off their lands. During this period she married Bryant Ward, a white trader, and was widely known thereafter as Nancy Ward. The couple ran an inn on Womankiller Creek in Tennessee. However, Nan'yehi returned to her birthplace, "Peace Town" or "Mother Town," in 1824 and died there among her own people. The Cherokee Nation would be without another female leader of such influence (and with few males of such influence) from 1824 until the late 1980s.

Today Nan'yehi is one of the most famous women in American colonial history and is often referred to simply as *the Ghighua* among the Cherokee. She has been periodically rediscovered as a powerful political and spiritual example by both Cherokee and non-Cherokee women. The Daughters of the American Revolution erected a memorial pyramid of quartz stones over her grave near Benton, Tennessee. A picture of her grave site can be seen on the Internet at www.cyberfair.gsn.org/pchs/Nancy_p.jpg. Allegedly, there is also a four- or five-foot statue commemorating her in the Arwine Cemetery in Grainger County, Tennessee.

For more information:

Noted anthropologist George Bird Grinnell twice interviewed E'hyoph'sta, once in 1908 and again in 1912, three years before her death. Most information on her comes from his accounts. To read them, see Grinnell, *The Fighting Cheyenne*, first published by the University of Oklahoma Press in 1915 and several times reprinted, and also his two volume set *The Cheyenne Indians: Their History and Ways of Life*, published by Yale University Press in 1923. The next recommended source on E'Hyoph'sta is Father Peter J. Powell's *People of the Sacred Mountain: A History of the Northern Cheyenne Chiefs and Warrior Societies, 1830-1879, with an Epilogue,1969-1974*, volumes 1 and 2, published by Harper & Row in 1981. Volume 1 includes on pages 134-135 an image entitled "A Woman Warrior," a picture from the Spotted Wolf-Yellow Nose Ledger. Powell hypothesizes that this is a representation of E'Hyoph'sta. No web sites containing information about her could be found.

Edwin Thompson Denig's *Five Indian Tribes of the Upper Missouri*, published by the University of Oklahoma Press in 1961, is the primary reference for the story of Woman Chief. There are several other works referring to her, but they are all built on Denig's material. These other sources include John C Ewers' "Deadlier than the Male," in *American Heritage*, volume XVI, number 4, June 1965, 10-13; Valerie Sherer Mather's "Native American Women in Medicine and the Military," *Journal of the West*, 21/2, 1982, 41-48; and Beatrice Medicine and Patricia Albers, eds., *The Hidden Half: Studies of Plains Indian Women*, published by the University Press of America in 1983. No web sites containing information about her could be found.

Most published information on the Crow woman known as the Other Magpie comes from oral testimony provided to Frank B. Linderman by Pretty Shield in the late 1920s. Pretty Shield's information was included in a book originally entitled *Red Mother*, first published in 1932. This was reprinted as *Pretty Shield: Medicine Woman of the Crows* by the John Day Company of New York in 1972. Two good general sources on the fighting at the Battle of the Rosebud are J. W. Vaughn's *With Crook at the Rosebud*, published by Stackpole in 1956, and Neil C. Mangum's *The Battle of the Rosebud: Prelude to the Little Bighorn*, published by Upton and Sons in 1987.

The Other Magpie is one of the most mysterious figures in Crow history. Carson Walks Over Ice, archivist at the Little Big Horn College on the Crow Reservation, told the author in a phone conversation on April 14, 1997, that the Other Magpie was not counted in the 1886 census of the Nation since her name does not appear on its rolls. Walks Over Ice feels positive that she married, changed her name before the census was taken (a not uncommon occurrence), and died childless. Had she had children there would be family history to add to other Crow oral tradition. In spite of years of searching, no other written records about her have been found.

However, articles by James S. Brust tell of a Western frontier photographer who may have captured in a single photograph both Osh Tisch and the Other Magpie. Dr. Brust and Mike Cowdrey have hypothesized that the Crow berdache labeled as "Squaw Jim" in the picture is actually Osh-Tisch and that the figure seated next to him is the Other Magpie. Crow historians have verified the identify of Osh-Tisch, but the lack of any documents or family history makes it next to impossible to positively identify the second person as the Other Magpie. The relevant articles by Brust are "Into the Face of History," *American Heritage*, volume 43, number 7 (November 1992), 104-113 and "John H. Fouch: First Photographer at Fort Keogh," *Montana, the Magazine of Western History*, volume 44, number 2 (May 1994), pp. 2-17. Other than Linderman's book on Pretty Shield, analysis of the photograph, and some additional Crow oral tradition, there are no other references on the Other Magpie. Internet searches returned 162 "hits" on the Other Magpie. However, all were for a science fiction story by R. Garcia y Robertson. Robertson's story is based on events in the spring and summer of 1876, and it parallels the Pretty Shield account.

Unlike the case of the Plains warriors above, hundreds of books contain references to Nan'yehi or Nancy Ward. Linda Grant De Pauw and Conover

Hunt's co-authored work *Remember the Ladies: Women in America 1750-1815*, published by Viking Press in 1976, is one of these. There is even a web site and hyperlink dedicated to Ward at www.nancyward.com, a site that warrants a visit for readers wanting more information.

I should also mention a few other women warriors, some with information on the Internet. These include Lozen and Gouyen of the Apache Nation (see www.peabody.harvard.edu/maria/Apachewomen.html; another site is www.peabody.harvard.edu/maria/Apachewomen.html); Running Eagle of the Blackfoot Nation (see www.whisperingwomen/nevnative/blackfoot.htm and www.whisperingwomen/nevnative/blackfoot.htm); Elk Hollering, also of the Blackfoot nation (no Internet search returns); and Throwing Down of the Shoshone nation (no Internet search returns). Sources on the history of women warriors may be available. More research is needed so that their stories can also be told.

NOTES

1. Powell, Father Peter J., *People of the Sacred Mountain: A History of the Northern Cheyenne Chiefs and Warrior Societies, 1830-1879, with an Epilogue, 1969-1974*, vol. I (San Francisco: Harper & Row, 1981), 577-578. The action is the one often known as "Beecher's Island." The primary source for this story is interviews conducted by George Bird Grinnell with E'hyoph'sta' on September 28, 1908. The Grinnell papers containing these interviews are archived in the Braun Research Library of the Southwest Museum in Los Angeles.

2. An informal treaty among the Upper Missouri Tribes was negotiated in parleys in Laramie, Wyoming, in 1851. Although no formal agreements were signed at the time, working arrangements and further overtures towards peace were made over the next several years. These efforts all eventually failed.

3. Denig, Edward Thompson, *Five Indian Tribes of the Upper Missouri: Sioux, Arickaras, Assiniboines, Crees, Crows* (Norman: University of Oklahoma Press, 1961), 195-200.

REVIEWS

Making Peace with Cochise: The 1872 Journal of Captain Joseph Alton Sladene, edited by Edwin R. Sweeney, with a Foreword by Frank J. Sladen, Jr. (Norman, Oklahoma: University of Oklahoma Press, 1997). Photographs, Foreword, appendix, notes, biblio., index, 179pp. Cloth. $24.95.

Captain Joseph Alton Sladen, who died in 1911, was aide de camp to Gen. Oliver Otis Howard throughout most of the Civil War and the Indian campaigns thereafter. The two officers had a lifelong friendship. A physician by training, Sladen was both observant and articulate in his duties as the general's aide. In 1872 Sladen recorded in a private journal the events leading to the final peacemaking with the famous Chiricahua Apache chief Cochise during the autumn of 1872.

The negotiations took place in the famous "West Stronghold" of the Dragoon Mountains, located in what is now the aptly named Cochise County in the southeastern corner of Arizona. Cochise had been involved in a raiding war against whites since 1860, when he was incited by the so-called Bascom Affair. The commanding views from the Dragoons above the Sulphur Springs and San Pedro valleys had given Cochise a strategic advantage because it had been easy for him to observe army activities at Fort Bowie in Apache Pass and elsewhere. By 1872 the aging chief was tired and eager to make peace. In one of the better known episodes of the Apache war, Chochise surrendered to General Howard at the Stronghold through the efforts of frontiersman Tom Jeffords. Cochise would later come to admire Howard, perhaps even more than Howard was admired by the chief, according to Sladen. In return for the chief's capitulation, Howard promised the Chiricahua Apaches that they would be allowed to remain in the familiar lands of today's Cochise County. Although those promises were eventually broken and the Chiricahuas were concentrated northward at the San Carlos Reservation, Cochise did not live to see their removal. The great leader's remains are buried today in his beloved Dragoon Mountains, a region of immense beauty (as this reviewer can attest from his explorations there in the 1970s while serving as a professor of history at Cochise College in Douglas).

Edwin R. Sweeney, Cochise's and Mangas Coloradas' biographer, obtained permission to edit and publish Sladen's journal from the captain's descendant, Frank J. Sladen, Jr. The journal is most illuminating because of Captain Sladen's vivid depiction not only of the peacemaking but also of the Apaches people and their impoverished and war-depleted existence in the Stronghold. Sladen often recounted the brutality of the Chiricahuas during the twelve-year war with the United States. But most interestingly—and highly unusually for whites who were writing accounts in the 1870s—Sladen nevertheless painted a vivid picture of individual Apaches as human beings. Attesting to their penchant for extreme cleanliness, honesty, sexual chastity, and especially the sense of humor exhibited through a cultural habit of playing practical jokes on one another, Sladen observed a side to the Indians that few of his generation saw or acknowledged.

Sladen's friendship with his "bueno amigo," Chochise's youngest son Naiche, then a teenaged boy, is especially heartwarming. Lightly clad, as were most of his band, Naiche would crawl under Sladen's blanket with Sladen at night to keep warm. (As a grown man, Naiche would ride with Geronimo and would be one of the last Chiricahuas to surrender when Geronimo submitted in 1886.)

Editor Sweeney's notes are extensive and knowledgeable, and his introduction and epilogue put Sladen's journal in full historical context. This important book is highly recommended both as original source documentation and as a very good read.

John H. Monnett   Metropolitan State College of Denver

American Indian Biographies, edited by Harvey Markowitz (Salem Press, Inc., Pasadena, 1999). Illus., time line, indexes, 436pp. Cloth. $55.00.

The Encyclopedia of Native American Biography: Six Hundred Life Stories of Important People, from Powhatan to Wilma Mankiller, by Bruce E. Johansen and Donald A. Grinde, Jr. (Da Capo Press, New York, 1998). Illus., Foreword, index, 464pp. Paper, $22.50.

The past five years have seen greatly increased interested in the United States and Canada in biographical reference works on the members of the continent's first nations. Two results of this interest are *American Indian Biographies* and the somewhat contrasting work *The Encyclopedia of Native American Biography.*

The 329 brief biographical sketches in *American Indian Biographies* are largely derived from the publisher's invaluable *Ready Reference: American Indians.* A wide range of persons are included, with the editor obviously taking pains to include women, activists, artists, authors and entertainers. However, as many as a third of all persons included had some role in a historic Indian conflict. The book is surprisingly strong in its coverage of Indians from the oft neglected European colonial and early U.S. periods and refreshingly inclusive of Canadian Indians and Métis. The work also does readers the service of providing most alternative names for each person.

Most entries in *American Indian Biographies* are under 500 words, though figures long or currently touted in American popular culture may be described in up to 3,000 words. Though most contributors are professional historians, the quality of the entries varies. Some authors, like Bruce E. Johansen, write authoritatively from their own research or from extensive reading. Others, such as one "independent scholar" who made errors in geographical descriptions in at least four entries, seem to have relied on a single secondary source or to have accepted old legends or contemporary rhetoric uncritically. Only a portion of the entries include a bibliography. *American Indian Biographies* is said to have been written and aimed at high school and undergraduate level. However, it can still be recommended to journal readers seeking a broadly inclusive, though not in-depth, ready reference on American Indians.

In contrast to *American Indian Biographies,* the reprinted *Encyclopedia of Native American Biography* leaves out the singers, painters, and poets of "popular history" in favor of including more of the military and political figures of "traditional" history. In addition to including a great many contemporary Indian activists, the *Encyclopedia* gives just due to a number of overlooked legal and religious reformers of the past. A few Americans of European descent who had significant interaction with Indians, such as George Custer and Elizabeth Cady Stanton, are also covered. In general, the more obscure individuals are dealt with in a single paragraph. The more influential persons are described in one- to four-page articles; many of these longer pieces include up-to-date listings of books and articles "for more information." A few of the articles contain conclusions that are arguable or use annoying cliches like "troops with itchy trigger fingers" (334). Still, the book delivers what its publisher promises, a considerable amount of useful information at a good price.

Allan N. York   Toronto, Ontario

America's National Historic Trails, by Kathleen Ann Cordes, with photographs by Jan Lammers. (Norman: University of Oklahoma Press, 1999). Illus., maps, appendices, index, 370pp. Paper. (Contact publisher for price.)

My public library's catalog lists 1,234 references to material on trails, 213 on national trails, 245 on the Oregon Trail, and 216 on the Santa Fe Trail. Why then was yet another book on trails published? *America's National Historic Trails* is different from most other titles in that it is a comprehensive guide to all twelve of the federally designated "national history trails." The National Trails System Act of 1868 eventually prompted the creation of eight national scenic trails, 800 national recreation trails, and twelve national historic trails. The latter are, in order of the date they were designated: Lewis and Clark Trail, Oregon Trail, Mormon Pioneer Trail, Idatarod Trail, Overland Mountain Trail, Nez Perce (Nee-Me-Poo) Trail, Santa Fe Trail, Trail of Tears, Juan Bautista de Anza Trail, California Trail, Pony Express Trail, and Selma to Montgomery Trail.

Author Kathleen Ann Cordes states that the purpose of her book is "to serve as an overall guide," and her work fulfills her purpose well. On average, she devotes twenty-eight pages to each historic route. Descriptions include the name and address of the administering agency, length in miles and kilometers, and the states through which each trail passes. The author provides a wealth of history in each chapter in an easily read style. Each history is followed by a very useful map, with each noteworthy location along the trail numbered and given a detailed description. In some cases, unfortunately—Trail of Tears in particular—the descriptions do not make it clear whether or not any features may still be seen at a location or whether the site is publicly accessible. Cordes also provides a bibliography for each entry which, at twelves citations per trail, is not extensive but is adequate.

For *Journal of the Indian Wars* readers, the book's attraction is the fact that ten of the twelve trails have direct or indirect associations with the Indian wars, and most of these have battlefields on or near the trail. Several battles were, in fact, the result of efforts to keep open the Oregon and Santa Fe Trails. Nez Perce (Nee-Me-Poo) Trail is of special interest as it is the direct result of an Indian war. Most Western history followers know of the Nez Perce flight from northeast Oregon to a point near Chinook, Montana, in 1877. Many groups have tried to accurately locate the exact course of the nearly 1,200 miles route. The first major engagement took place when the Nez Perce fought the U.S. army and civilian volunteers in White Bird Canyon, near Idaho's Salmon River, on the morning of June 17, 1877. From there, the pursuit began, ending 110 days later on October 5 when Chief Joseph, as the representative of the refugee Nez Perce, surrendered. The appropriate map and its accompanying site descriptions allow one to follow closely the trail by automobile.

America's National Historic Trails is not intended to be a hiker's guide, and specific local directions are seldom provided. It does, however, provide very good background texts and general descriptions. Those who want to become familiar with the historic trail system and perhaps one day actually to retrace the trails by car won't go wrong by beginning their quest with this book.

Connie O'Sullivan   Houston, TX

The Politics of Hallowed Ground: Wounded Knee and the Struggle for Indian Sovereignty, by Maro Gonzalez and Elizabeth Cook-Lynn (Urbana: University of Illinois Press, 1998). Photos, maps, index, 360pp. Cloth, $39.95. Paper, $19.95.

As the granddaughter of Dakota Territory pioneers, this reviewer found *The Politics of Hallowed Ground* to be a fascinating opening into a world I never knew growing up in South Dakota, a world seldom viewed by non-Indians. In 1890, Big Foot's off-reservation band of Lakota was confronted by the U.S. Seventh Cavalry and decimated in and following a fight that took the lives of many Indian women and children. In the view of the Lakota, Dakota, and Nakota Sioux nations, the "incident" (as non-Indian historians have blandly termed it) is a "crime against humanity for which the government must be indicted." This book is about the Wounded Knee Survivor Association's work to extract justice from the United States in the form of a formal apology for the event and recognition of the site as a unique national monument to be named "Wounded Knee National Tribal Park." Oglala Lakota counselor Mario

Gonzales, the attorney for the association, kept a diary as he worked with group members to draft legislation that they hoped would be passed for the 100th anniversary of the massacre. Ten years later, that legislation has still not been enacted, and the government, instead of an apology, has issued only their weak "deep regrets."

Working from Gonzales' diary, Yankton and Dakota writer Elizabeth Cook-Lynn skillfully weaves a "chronicle" that brings together the historical and legal context of the massacre with the ongoing struggle to make the United States government own up to its atrocities and its obligations. Her commentary and analysis begin with the European colonial concept called the "doctrine of discovery," a doctrine that later was used to justify the theft of Dakota and Lakota land and, ultimately, the Wounded Knee Massacre. In her view, the relationship of the U.S. to native people remains that of colonizer. She continues throughout the book to drive home with relentless clarity the thesis that "the United States has sought to destroy Native American culture and nationalism, not only on the battlefields in past centuries but also through its political and legal institutions from the time of the Declaration of Independence in 1776 up to the present. . . ." According to Cook-Lynn, after the late nineteenth and early twentieth century policy of forced assimilation failed, the government moved to a contemporary attempt to hide the power dynamic behind meaningless calls for "multiculturism and diversity." (The republic's lip-service commitment to a government based on the consent of the people has always been apparent to those denied their voice: black Americans and women, for example.) The book offers a significant transformation in perspective by addressing and exposing the real goal of U.S. Indian policies, the goal of control. In this publication, Cook-Lynn follows, from the inside, specific examples of the U.S. government's denial of native nations' sovereign right to choose who will make their laws and of the systematic attempt to destroy their sovereignty.

The structure of *The Politics of Hallowed Ground* is unusual and serves as an invitation into the heart of Lakota and Dakota culture. The reader learns about the chain of events leading to the present struggle from a multiplicity of perspectives within the Sioux nations. In this and other ways, readers are invited to participate in traditional Sioux methods of oral discourse. As Cook-Lynn deftly interweaves personal with political history, anecdotes carry equal weight with historical and legal documents. In addition, while Euro-American history is written in the belief that time passes in a linear fashion and what is past is past,

Cook-Lynn writes from an Indian perspective in which past and present circle one another, both existing in the moment.

Cook-Lynn summarizes the book's course and aims best in the epilogue: "*The Politics of Hallowed Ground* is a modern accounting of the efforts of ordinary people to make sense of colonial politics in our time and it follows a paper trail as clear and unmistakable as the trail of blood left in the hills of the Pine Ridge Reservation after the killing a century ago. The expectation of the current effort narrated here is that crimes against humanity can be acknowledged by their perpetrators, that official apologies can ensue, that stolen lands and rights can be returned to tribal peoples, that colonization and enforced assimilation can be identified as among the historical crimes against humanity, and that the recognition of wrongful death can be more than just an ache in the heart."

Sally Roesch Wagner, Aberdeen, South Dakota; Director of the Matilda Joslyn Gage Foundation, Fayetteville, New York

McIntosh and Weatherford, Creek Indian Leaders, by Benjamin W. Griffith, Jr. (Tuscaloosa, AL: University of Alabama Press, 1988). Illus., map, Preface, notes, biblio., index, 322pp. Paper, $19.95.

Author Benjamin W. Griffith, Jr.'s *McIntosh and Weatherford* provides a dual biography of two southeastern Indian leaders born of Creek [Muskogee] mothers and Scottish fathers in the late eighteenth century. Despite their common ancestries, William McIntosh and William Weatherford followed different paths in their adult lives. Weatherford, raised in the more traditional and nativistic Upper Creek towns, became a leader of the Red Sticks and fought against the United States in the disastrous Creek War from 1813 to 1814. McIntosh came from the more acculturated Lower Creek towns and fought alongside the United States in both the Creek War and First Seminole War in 1818. His close relationships with politicians in Washington and Georgia and his willingness to sell them the Creek homeland became his undoing. After signing away millions of acres to the United States in 1825 without the approval of the Creek leadership, his fellow tribesmen assassinated McIntosh.

Griffith has produced a book that is well written and well researched, but there are several flaws, the most glaring of which is the uneven treatment of his subjects. McIntosh receives far more coverage than Weatherford, who virtually disappears after the Battle of Horseshoe Bend and does not appear again until the end of the book in a short passage summarizing his life from 1814 to his death in 1824. Little is known about their early lives, and the author addresses this dilemma by providing an overview of Creek Indian culture and child-rearing practices to fill this void. Nevertheless, the reader does really not meet either man until each is an adult.

These significant gaps are indicative of the problems historians often face when writing the biographies of historical Indian persons; thus, Griffith cannot be faulted for tackling the life stories of McIntosh and Weatherford despite these obstacles. However, he would have been more successful to simply change the premise of his book so that it promises what it ultimately delivers. Rather than being a dual biography, Griffith's book is a history of the Creeks during the early nineteenth century that uses the lives of McIntosh and Weatherford as organizational themes.

These are relatively minor criticisms, and students of southeastern Indian history will find much that is useful. Griffith does a very good job presenting the history of the Creek Indians during this tumultuous period of their history. The story is made more personal and interesting with the biographical sketches of McIntosh and Weatherford that emerge and the fine overview of Creek Indian culture and society that Griffith provides. For these reasons, it is an excellent book for use in undergraduate courses.

Patrick J. Jung   Marquette University

Fort Laramie and the Great Sioux War, by Paul L. Hedren (Norman: University of Oklahoma Press, 1998). Illus., maps, preface, appendix, biblio., index, 313pp. Paper, $15.95.

Fort Laramie and the Great Sioux War was originally published in hardcover and titled *Fort Laramie in 1876: Chronicle of a Frontier Post at War*. In this recent paperback edition, author Paul Hedren has provided additional information on the role played by Fort Laramie in the months of 1876-1877 and on some of the personalities associated with the post's activities at the time.

Hedren enthusiastically seeks to provide an even more detailed understanding of the post's part in the Great Sioux War of War of 1876 than in the first edition. Prior to the publication of Hedren's work, histories of Fort Laramie had focused mainly on the Grattan Fight ("Massacre") of 1876, the 1860s Bozeman Trail conflicts, and the 1868 treaty made nearby with the Sioux.

Following extensive research, the author states that he "discovered a multifaceted story of Fort Laramie in 1876 that proved to be uncommonly dramatic." Hedren makes a case for the strategic value of the fort in the 1870s as a transportation crossroads and a source of logistical support and supplies to the frontier army. With a smooth writing style, Hedren gives the reader a good snapshot of life at what was one of the most important posts in the West. Readers will encounter a host of fascinating characters, from the famous, like George Crook, "Wild Bill" Hickok, "Buffalo Bill" Cody, Asa Carr, Wesley Merritt, Phil Sheridan, and Ranald Mackenzie, to the little known "support cast" of 1876, including "Teddy" Egan, John Collins, Elizabeth Burt, and many others. Hedren also captures the emotions of the individuals and families at the post in that year—the sorrow over the death of a family members, the desperation of destitute miners from the Black Hills, the agony of wives worrying about soldier husbands in the field.

Hedren also briefly covers Fort Laramie history to the starting point of the Sioux War, the issuing of instructions to the Sioux to return to their reservation by January 31, 1876, or be considered hostile. An entire chapter is devoted the to geography of the conflict, explaining in this way how and why Fort Laramie was to play an important strategic role. Other chapters deal with the preparations made to carry the campaign to the Indians, including the growing quartermaster and commissary activities needed for George Crook's expeditions and the arrival of new troops at the post. More than sixty maps and photographs provide additional incentive to read Hedren's work.

This fine documentary of the role of Fort Laramie in a decisive conflict is recommended reading for both the novice and the knowledgeable Indian wars enthusiast.

Ron Nichols   Costa Mesa, California

Massacre at Cheyenne Hole: Lieutenant Austin Henely and the Sappa Creek Controversy, by John H. Monnett (Boulder: University Press of Colorado, 1999). Illus., map, intro., appendix, biblio., index, 143pp. Cloth, $24.95.

With his latest contribution in the field, *Massacre at Cheyenne Hole*, John Monnett builds upon his reputation as an author who provides a dispassionate, objective examination of the history of Indian wars despite the bewildering tangle of emotional issues raised in this heyday of revisionist history. The author is clearly not one to shy from taking on a difficult and politically charged issue. This time he takes on the controversy surrounding a brief skirmish between elements of the Sixth U.S. Cavalry and a village of Indians who had camped on the Middle Fork of Sappa Creek in Kansas Territory. The affair was the sad conclusion of a flight by a band composed mostly of Southern Cheyenne, from the Cheyenne-Arapaho Reservation in present-day Oklahoma. From that morning of April 23, 1875, down to the present day, this confrontation at the very end of the "Buffalo War" (Red River War) on the Southern Plains has been shrouded in controversy, half-truths, and misshapen political agendas. Monnett sets out to settle the dust, while he remains painfully aware that he won't be settling it once and for all.

In the years following the fight, young Lt. Austin Henely—who led the Sixth Cavalry's attack out of Fort Wallace—was considered a hero in the West, as were the eight troopers from his H Company who received of the Medal of Honor for their bravery and courage in the clash. It wasn't until three decades later that intimations surfaced claiming that the Sappa Creek skirmish was a massacre and that Little Bull had attempted to surrender to the soldiers. Tales of innocent Cheyenne women and children being murdered, some even burned alive in the destruction of the lodges, became commonplace by the first of the twentieth century. Still, such rumor and innuendo of a massacre of "innocents" at Sappa Creek did not receive a wide press for some eighty years. As Monnett shows, it was not until 1953 with the publication of Mari Sandoz's *Cheyenne Autumn* that sketchy and unsubstantiated reports of atrocities committed by Lieutenant Henely's men began to gain wider notice. By that time, the rumors reached a more sympathetic audience, detached not only from that time in our nation's history but also from the cultural "sense of place" formerly inherent in most who live "beyond the wide Missouri."

The shameful drubbing Sandoz gave the Sixth Cavalry was but the beginning of a campaign of misinformation and outright lies which was encouraged by the 1958 publication of the reminiscences of Sgt. Frederick Platten. Ironically, Platten had been one of the men who had received the Medal of Honor for the action at Sappa Creek. Though others would later embellish his story in an attempt to mold the controversy to fit their own aims, to this day Platten's version remains the only firsthand report to ever begin to suggest atrocities might have occurred.

Then the Sappa Creek controversy entered a new phase, an era of social reconstruction and historical revisionism. With the 1960s and 1970s, the United States plummeted through soul-searching as it waged an interminable war against an impoverished agrarian nation in Southeast Asia. Condemnation of this latter-day twentieth century struggle provided a model for judging the country's historical past, particularly the period in which the country went about pacifying the Great Plains for white settlement. The Vietnam era was also the era of the emergence of "Red Power" and the American Indian Movement, which was aware of the power of the memories of the tragedies at Sand Creek and Wounded Knee. It was only natural that the skirmish at Sappa Creek came to be viewed, in Monnett's words, as "a Sand Creek Massacre in microcosm," referring to the 1864 atrocity that few would ever seek to defend. Given a heightened symbolic significance for Sappa Creek, it did not take long for all of the contentious literature on the subject to fall completely into a "pro-Henely" or an "anti-Henely" camp.

Part of the problem, as this reviewer has found in conducting research for his novels, is that much of the history and historical fiction written over the past thirty years is of a absolutist nature. An event and its characters are often recast into a good versus evil morality tale akin to the epic of some ancient Arthurian battle. Great moral lessons are to be found, supposedly, in small, brief, less than historically significant events. Rather then permitting participants in events from being merely human beings, ordinary people are represented as symbols of what is loathsome about our nation's story.

Monnett's book also causes me to wonder how members of tribes raised to practice unremitting hatred and brutality against traditional enemies came within the space of one generation to be represented as fault-free, downtrodden people innocent themselves of committing atrocities. Also, why are events contemporaneous to Sappa Creek in which whites were brutalized and murdered known only to a very few of the best-read students and researchers of history? What of the Hennessey wagon train attack? What about the butchery committed against Oliver Short's survey party in the Lost Valley massacre? What of the heartrending story of the attack on the Germany family in southwestern Kansas, with its elements of torture, rape, murder, continued when the four German sisters were carried off into concubinage and slavery among the Southern Cheyenne?

Despite the layers of confusion, suspicion, and selective memory now complicating the story of Henely's attack, Monnett manages to shine a bright light on this dark corner of western history. He does this not so much by explaining what might have occurred on Sappa Creek in the spring of 1875 but by explaining how the story has been distorted by those with a desire to rewrite history in their own image. [Note: Readers interested in a military history of the engagement are referred to William Y. Chalfant's excellent 1997 work, *Cheyennes at Dark Water Creek.*] After exhaustive research into the controversy, Monnett explores the conflicting testimony and moves on to explain why and how this divergent and emotionally charged testimony exists. He provides a compact case study showing how, as new life was continually breathed into the controversy, changing interpretation of the event illuminated American's evolving perceptions of the Indian wars. He demonstrates how important it is to ascertain the motivations affecting historians' methodology and conclusions.

Every new generation, it seems, will take up the cause of a past generation as a means of fighting new battles. When this happens, the truth very often becomes drowned out in all the shouting. Monnett's *Massacre at Cheyenne Hole* is recommended reading for all those seeking to understand how to separate historical dialogue from noisy static.

Terry Johnston   Billings, MT

In Custer's Shadow: Major Marcus A. Reno, by Ronald H. Nichols, introduction by Brian C. Pohanka (Fort Collins, CO: Old Army Press, 1999), Volume 15 in the Source Custeriana Series, xii, illus., maps, intro., notes, appendices, index, 407pp. Cloth, $35.00. Order from Broken Arrow Books, 3131 Monroe Way, Costa Mesa, CA 92626-2826; California residents add 7.75% tax.

It has often been observed that military disasters invariably produce a search for culprits. The Battle of the Little Bighorn, fought and lost by the U.S. Army in Montana Territory on June 25-26, 1876, is no exception to this generalization. Just as the Monday-morning quarterback second guesses the decisions of the coach who "lost" Sunday's football game, so efforts were made within the military shortly after the battle to explain the defeat of Lt. Col. George Armstrong Custer and the Seventh U.S. Cavalry at the hands of the Lakota Sioux and their Northern Cheyenne allies. Many held Custer responsible for what the expedition commander, Brig. Gen. Alfred H. Terry, reputedly called a "sad and terrible blunder." Others, notably Custer's friends and admirers, blamed his subordinates for the tragedy on the Little Bighorn.

Among those held accountable was the senior surviving officer of the battle, Maj. Marcus A. Reno. As Custer's second-in-command, Reno's conduct and actions came under fire in the debate which followed the disaster. Charges of cowardice, dereliction of duty, and intoxication came after Reno's disorderly retreat from the Little Bighorn valley at the opening of the battle. His later failure to charge the Indian encampment in response to the "sound of guns" from Custer's immediate command farther west also led to criticism. Custer's West Point classmate and Civil War foe, Thomas L. Rosser, charged that Reno "took refuge in the hills, and abandoned Custer and his gallant comrades to their fate!" Reno's earliest biographer, Frederick Whittaker, flatly attributed Custer's defeat to "Reno's incapacity."

Had he not played a role at the Little Bighorn, Marcus Reno would probably have lived and died in obscurity, destined to share with so many officers in the Civil War and frontier army a solid, if unspectacular, career out of the public eye. If the disaster guaranteed Reno a place in history, it also obscured the man as he labored under the burden of Custer and his last battle. Ultimately Reno failed to restore his tarnished reputation, despite a court of inquiry decision in 1879 exonerating his actions on that bloody Sunday. Reno, too, became a "casualty" of the Little Bighorn.

In the partisan debate stemming from the battle, many have come to Reno's defense. However, such advocates of the major's case as Frederic F. van de Water, Fred Dustin, and E. A. Brininstool simply demonstrated their hostility towards Custer the "Glory Hunter" at the expense of historical objectivity and even truth. Semi-fictionalized biographies such as *The Convenient Coward* and *Faint the Trumpet Sounds*, no matter how well written, have further distorted our perception of Reno and these events. The time has long been ripe for a comprehensive, well-researched, objective biography of the man who lived in Custer's shadow.

Ronald Nichols has met this challenge. This was no simple task, as Reno is not an attractive personality with whom one could easily identify or empathize. He not only failed to inspire colleagues, but also alienated those who would defend him. A West Point classmate, Cyrus Comstock, recorded in his diary, "Reno is not very popular." Others noted his aggressive behavior. Akin to the French national scapegoat Captain Dreyfus a generation later, Reno was not an ideal person to defend.

Nichols knows his subject well. His biography is the product of more than fifteen years of diligent research, which led the author to such diverse parts of the U.S. as Illinois, Pennsylvania, and South Carolina in search of little known primary source material. Such far-flung sources complement the extensive use of military records in the National Archives, U.S. Military Academy, and U.S. Army Military History Institute, as well as the files of the Little Bighorn Battlefield National Monument. One result of this exemplary research is new evidence which establishes that General Terry never intended or expected Reno's dismissal from the army as a result of his court-martial in 1880. An impressive array of maps and illustrations (including the first known photographs of Reno) enhance the book's credibility.

A complete and balanced picture of Reno's life emerges from the author's efforts. We learn not only of Reno's varied and accomplished service in the Civil War and his role at the Little Big Horn. We also witness his experiences as a young man in Illinois, a cadet at West Point, a newly commissioned lieutenant on the frontier before the Civil War, a major in the Seventh Cavalry on Reconstruction duty in the South, a commander of the Northern Boundary Survey military escorts, and a member of the small arms board which adopted the Springfield breech loading system as the standard weapon for the U.S. Army for a generation. Ironically, the quirks of the Springfield carbine carried by Custer's troops also played a role in the debate as to the causes of the Custer disaster.

Complementing this story are insights which occasionally shed light on Reno's personality and the turmoil in his life after the Little Bighorn. Above all, the death of his wife, Mary Hannah, which occurred while he was in the field with the Northern Boundary Survey in 1874, was a devastating blow. Noting her positive counter effect on Reno's aloof and abrasive demeanor, Nichols concludes that the major "would find it difficult in later years to socialize in the close knit society of the army post." The emotional impact of this personal loss explains, if not justifies, Reno's later behavior and probable alcoholism.

The author has avoided the temptation to focus on Reno's role at the Little Bighorn at the expense of other events in that officer's life. He has written this biography in such an even-handed, factual manner that the uninformed reader would not be aware of the author's publicly avowed sympathies for his subject. Nichols has avoided controversial value judgments. Perhaps his readers would have been better served if he had provided in-depth analysis and opinions on issues worthy of debate. Reno's alleged intoxication and rumored proposal to abandon the wounded at the Little Bighorn come to mind. An evaluation of Reno's relationship with Custer and other officers of the Seventh Cavalry might have resolved undocumented allegations of factionalism and hostility within the regiment.

If there is a flaw in this important contribution to the study of the Indian wars, it is the chapters dealing with the Little Bighorn. Perhaps the shortsightedness found there reflects the focus of the reviewer. Nichols' account of the battle has clearly relied on the conflicting testimony at the Reno Court of Inquiry in 1879 to the virtual exclusion of other primary sources, notably Walter M. Camp's interviews and correspondence with survivors of the battle. The author's unconditional faith in the court's record is at odds with those who believe its proceedings were a whitewash. One need read only the testimony of Capt. Frederick W. Benteen to find clear evidence of misrepresentation, if not deliberate fabrication, at the inquiry. Given these facts, the biography adds little to the vast literature on the battle. Finally, the absence of a bibliography deprives those who passionately study the subject of a valuable reference tool.

However, such omissions are not fatal given the author's in-depth research and commitment to providing "a full picture of Reno the man and the soldier." Overall, Ronald Nichols has succeeded in his objective and provided "a fair and accurate picture of a truly complex 19th century soldier." *In Custer's Shadow* belongs in the library of every serious student of the Indian wars as well as Custer and the Little Bighorn.

C. Lee Noyes   Morrisonville, New York

Utah's Black Hawk War, by John Alton Peterson. (Salt Lake City: University of Utah Press, 1998). Illus., maps, notes, biblio., index, 432pp. Paper, $19.95.

John Alton Peterson's *Utah's Black Hawk War* is a comprehensively researched, engaging narrative history that will be of interest to many readers of *Journal of the Indian Wars*. The book is a thorough examination of a little-known 1865-72 conflict in post-Civil War Utah Territory between Latter Day Saints (LDS or "Mormon") settlers and a dissident band of Indians under the leadership of the determined Ute warrior Antonga, also known as Black Hawk. Peterson aptly chronicles the events and military engagements of this protracted war and untangles the complex relationships between Mormons, Indians, and non-Mormon government officials.

Despite these evident positive qualities, the book suffers from two significant defects, not the least of which is a peculiar analytical framework which derives from the author's need to engage in the ongoing historiographical debate over LDS-Indian relations. His argument holds that LDS settlers, influenced by church leaders and Book of Mormon doctrines, enjoyed better relations with Indians than existed in surrounding territories, a bizarre interpretation that perhaps owes more to the driving force of contemporary LDS propaganda than to historical inquiry. The premise is also a rather slippery one, a kind of comparative argument without the comparison, since Peterson does not examine Indian relations elsewhere. But even *if* the point is conceded, the text makes it abundantly clear that the difference in relations is only a matter of degree. The author admits that while Utah's LDS settlers might not have possessed the same genocidal fury as their gold rush counterparts in California or Colorado or exhibited the same Indian-hating tendencies as John M. Chivington's cadres, the outcome of the confrontation in Utah was every bit as disastrous for Utah's Indians.

The author is at pains to exonerate Brigham Young's role in the Black Hawk conflict. He extensively quotes Young's epistles to his subordinates, even italicizing the most beatific passages, all in the attempt to demonstrate that Young and his followers at least meant well. Yet, Peterson also recounts numerous Mormon atrocities, for example, the slaughter of Timpanogos Utes during the Fort Utah conflict and the subsequent severing of "40 or 50" of their heads, the calculated murder of non-belligerent Indian hostages in the Mormon villages of Nephi and Moroni, the massacre of terrified Paiute captives in Circleville, and much more.

The book's second defect concerns the inescapable selectivity in Peterson's presentation of evidence. The author cannot hide the perspective of LDS-apologia in his narrative (though he tries hard to do so.) Virtually all of his source material is derived from the correspondence of Utah settlers and officials, the vast majority of it from church members. Thus he unerringly perpetuates the LDS viewpoints on every significant issue. Peterson also adopts the conventional LDS language of discourse—e.g., non-Mormons become "gentiles," Mormons are "Saints," and Indians are occasionally rendered as "Lamanites" (Book of Mormon style)—while ignoring contemporary anthropological methodologies and making only the slightest use of Ute oral traditions. Everything is refracted through the lens of the LDS pioneer narrative portrayed as objective history by a LDS historian.

In his tortured conclusion, Peterson grudgingly acknowledges what is already abundantly clear to dispassionate readers: LDS members drove Indians out of their homelands, destroyed their subsistence base, and met armed resistance with conquering force. But finding these realities disturbingly hard to accept, he retreats yet again to a recitation of Brigham Young's good intentions. In a last ditch attempt to provide a comparative framework for his rationalized and shaded interpretations, the author inaccurately compares isolated events of the Black Hawk War to the 1864 Sand Creek massacre. A much better comparison might have been made to LDS complicity in Edward Connor's 1863 massacre of approximately 275 Northwestern Shoshone at Bear River. Peterson also inaccurately concludes that "when Indians got out of line" in other territories, they were "quickly destroyed by federal forces" while LDS members killed the Indians less quickly and less systematically. Nonetheless, they killed them.

Warren Metcalf   University of Oklahoma

INDEX

Fine Military Books from Upton & Sons

The Custer Mystery, by Charles G. Du Bois. New printing. A fine analysis of the development of the Battle of the Little Bighorn, and especially the portion of the field involving Custer and his five troops. This study is so perceptively written readers may suspect author du Bois was actually there. Introduction by the late Dr. Lawrence A. Frost. *The Custer Mystery* will satisfy and stimulate even the most advanced Indian War specialist, as well as general readers. Photos, rosters, maps, and index. ISBN 0-912783-06-0. Cloth, d.j., 198pp. $35.00

VOLUME 4, MONTANA AND THE WEST SERIES

"This is a serious study, as only a handful are, and entitled to respectful, thoughtful attention." Robert M. Utley, noted historian

General Terry's Last Statement to Custer, by John S. Manion. The first printing of an edition originally published in 1983 as a 51-page booklet. Manion's account answers questions raised in the original (and hard-to-find) paper printing. According to the author, there were *two* Adams sisters, and Mary Adams was present on the *Far West* when Custer was given verbal orders by General Terry. Furthermore, it was Maria Adams who was present at Fort Lincoln when the news of the disaster at the Little Bighorn reached that post. *General Terry's Last Statement* is one of the most interesting and original research project of recent years. Photos, illustrations, maps, index. ISBN 0-912783-33-8. Cloth, d.j., 182pp. $37.50

Benteen's Scout to the Left: The Route From the Divide to the Morass, June 25, 1876, by Roger Darling. This unique title was originally published in 1987 in a small printing of 500 copies. On June 25, 1876, Custer divided his command, ordering Captain Benteen to scout to the left in search of the Indian village. Darling's study meticulously examines that aspect of the campaign. He drove and walked the route, reconciling official reports with times and distances. Bound in linen with gold stamping, this edition includes 21 photos, 10 diagrams, large folding map and endpaper maps, notes, and index. ISBN 0-912783-08-7. 8 ½ x 11, 120pp. $75.00

VOLUME 1, CUSTER TRAILS SERIES

UPTON AND SONS, PUBLISHERS, 917 Hillcrest Street, El Segundo, California 90245
Web Site: www.uptonbooks.com / E-Mail: richardupton@worldnet.att.net
FREE CATALOG / ORDER: 800-959-1876 / Fax: 310-322-4739

The Western Heritage Institute Presents

General Crook's 1876 Campaign Against the Sioux
(August 24-26, 2000)

This truly unique program features

John D. McDermott
award winning author and lecturer

Tour the key sites of the Campaign:

▲ **Reynolds' Fight**
▲ **The Rosebud Battle**
▲ **A Walking Tour of the Dull Knife Fight**

Plus, participate in a firearms demonstration by noted authority and collector Bob Edwards

Eyewitness accounts will be dramatically brought to life by presentations from Mr. McDermott, as well as Crow, Sioux, and Cheyenne seminar leaders and seminar participants!

Registration, limited to 20 participants, includes four nights' accomodations at the historic TA Ranch, food, battlefield tours and entertainment.

Inquiries welcome! Call toll free 1-800-368-7398, or write to us at P.O. Box 313, Buffalo, Wyoming 82834
Visit us on the web at www.taranch.com